FRAGILE

A Christian Perspective on
Overcoming Unhealthy Thoughts

B.T. Semeschuk M. Th.

Unless otherwise indicated, all Scripture quotations taken from the New King James Version®. Copyright © 1982 by Thomas Nelson. Used by permission. All rights reserved. Scripture quotations marked (NLT) are taken from the Holy Bible, New Living Translation, copyright ©1996, 2004, 2007, 2013, 2015 by Tyndale House Foundation. Used by permission of Tyndale House Publishers, Inc., Carol Stream, Illinois 60188. All rights reserved. Scripture quotations marked (MSG) are taken from THE MESSAGE, copyright © 1993, 1994, 1995, 1996, 2000, 2001, 2002 by Eugene H. Peterson. Used by permission of NavPress. All rights reserved. Represented by Tyndale House Publishers, Inc. Scripture quotations marked (CEV) are from the Contemporary English Version Copyright © 1991, 1992, 1995 by American Bible Society. Used by Permission. Scripture quotations marked (GNT) are from the Good News Translation in Today's English Version- Second Edition Copyright © 1992 by American Bible Society. Used by Permission. Scripture quotations marked (MKJV) taken from the Modern King James Version of the Holy Bible. Copyright © 1962–1998 by J.P. Green Sr. Used by permission of the copyright holder. Scripture quotations marked (NASB) taken from the New American Standard Bible® (NASB), Copyright © 1960, 1962, 1963, 1968, 1971, 1972, 1973, 1975, 1977, 1995 by The Lockman Foundation. Used by permission. www.Lockman.org. Scripture quotations marked (KJV) taken from the Holy Bible, King James Version, which is in the public domain.

Printed in Canada
ISBN: 978-1-4866-1551-3

Word Alive Press
131 Cordite Road, Winnipeg, MB R3W 1S1
www.wordalivepress.ca

Cataloguing in Publication information may be obtained through Library and Archives Canada

I would like to dedicate this book to my wife, Cheryl.
You are my dearest and most cherished treasure.
Forever, I am grateful to you,
my high school sweetheart.

"A man's greatest treasure is his wife
—she is a gift from the Lord."
(Proverbs 18:22, CEV)

Foremost I want to publically thank my Lord and Savior, without whom I would not have even attempted this assignment. His love, leading, and wisdom are far beyond my natural ability. Thank you, Jesus.

CONTENTS

PREFACE

ONE AFTERNOON I RECEIVED AN UNDERSTANDING OF SEVEN things that make people fragile. In an upstairs bedroom that I used for my office, I was asking God questions, looking for answers to some of the same questions we all have.

"Why are things that I think need to change, not changing?" I asked. "Why, God, when you can do anything, do you not seem to be doing what I think is good for me?"

I glanced into the open closet and noticed an empty box sitting on the top shelf. The bottom of the box showed through the wire shelf, and it read "Fragile." Looking at the word, I heard this question spoken within me: "Are you a fragile Christian?"

I stopped and immediately thought, *What does that mean?*

With barely any hesitation, my spirit quickened and I was shown an acronym for the word fragile. I immediately understood that these areas in my life had the power to make me fragile.

Fear

Rejection

Anxiety

Guilt

Intimidation

Lies

Excuses

In a moment, I understood that these seven factors affect us all, withholding the richness life has to offer. God does not withhold anything; rather, our reactions to these seven things are the culprits.

As the years went by, I noticed that every one of these feelings has caused me to react in a certain way. Their negative influence affects our judgment and decision-making processes. They become engrained in us and change who we really are. Their seemingly invisible strength stops us from accomplishing the very things we were created to accomplish.

As with me, you will find that some traits of fragility are more predominant than others. Some will have more impact and a greater negative influence than others.

However, I began to work on each one to overcome its sway in my life.

This book cannot contain all the discernment and knowledge these emotions might conjure up within us. Every person will be affected to a varying degree and face their own personal battle. For me, it seems that all these traits have been in effect at one time or another in my life. Even today I need to stay mindful of these fragilities.

In this book, I have described and explained these fragilities to the best of my ability, as I see them. I have also included teachings from the Bible that can help us overcome the emotional states they produce.

Exact definitions between peoples and dictionaries are not policed by any universal authority. This means that you may interpret these words differently than I do at first glance. My prayer is that as you read this book, God will reveal these truths as He did for me. I believe you will be enlightened and empowered to overcome, finding your place of peace.

It is no coincidence that you picked up this book! Let it be a launching pad in your journey to overcoming wrong beliefs about yourself. From my own experience, just understanding these principles has been an important step in helping to cut through the confusion and disappointment of life.

Fragile means delicate, frail, brittle, and easily broken.

INTRODUCTION:
Identity

*These things I have spoken to you, that in Me
you may have peace. In the world you will
have tribulation; but be of good cheer, I have
overcome the world.*

(John 16:33)

IT ISN'T POSSIBLE TO RECEIVE HELP WITHOUT FIRST
understanding that feelings can control one's personality,
attitudes, decisions, and serenity. This book is not
intended to protect feelings or shelter a person from
their effects. In order to become whole, the Band-Aid
that covers up our hurts needs to be ripped off to expose
what is underneath.

Let's begin with an explanation of what it means to
be fragile.

THE WORLD'S WAY

It seems increasingly evident that people are not at peace.
There is unrest and instability in our homes, relationships,
and communities. The world's answer to these excessive

and extreme feelings has been to accept them as normal. A secular life coach, counselor, or psychologist will find it difficult to tell you that your reactions to such feelings are unnatural. Their action plans often contain advice on how to accept feelings rather than change them, or even asphyxiate them when necessary.

This leaves people with the belief that they will never have peace. They begin to believe they're stuck in a world that's more powerful than they can handle. This frustration grows even though they instinctually know this isn't true, that we can find peace in this life.

THE BEST WAY

This book wasn't written for atheists. To get help, you need to believe that God created us, and that belief also needs to include the goodness of God. I would encourage everyone to judge for themselves the truths found in Scripture. For me, the truth is clear. Only when we are able to overcome can we be free to achieve our destiny and enjoy the fullness of life.

The words of Jesus Christ must be taken at face value. We can find rest and harmony in our mental state. Jesus very clearly referred to the events of today when He said, *"These things I have spoken to you, that in Me you may have peace. In the world you will have tribulation; but be of good cheer, I have overcome the world"* (John 16:33).

CAN WE SEE IT?

Knowing these seven fragilities—fear, rejection, anxiety, guilt, intimidation, lies, and excuses—and recognizing their effects can be two completely separate matters. Some will fail to see the consequences of these fragilities in their lives. It seems easy to recognize them in others, but in themselves they believe they have little influence. Or so they think.

On the other hand, some will see that these fragilities have hindered their progress towards a peaceful and successful life. They will acknowledge them as major obstacles to their freedom. This acknowledgment is a big first step.

SENTIMENTS

Many people today, even Christians, seem to be controlled by their feelings. These feelings end up controlling their decisions, their choices, and even their futures, leaving them fragile.

> People believe that feelings are such a powerful force that they cannot be changed or wrong.

The word fragile is defined as delicate, frail, brittle, and easily broken. These frailties are all linked to our sentiments, which are our beliefs and judgments, and they usually aren't founded on any certainty.

People believe that feelings are such a powerful force that they cannot be changed or wrong. They believe that fear, rejection, anxiety, guilt, intimidation, lies, and excuses are just sensations we have to live with. My prayer is that everyone begins to see that feelings are from God, intended to bring wholeness.

However, in extreme cases they become a snare and a thief to one's contentment.

FEELINGS DO EXIST

We all know feelings exist because everyone has felt every one of them. Anyone who has lived more than a couple of years has had opportunity to sense feelings. Our feelings affect us emotionally, mentally, and even physically. If you believe that God designed us, then you must surely believe in feelings. God designed them for a purpose.

I've had many opportunities to see feelings at work in others. Being a senior pastor, a student pastor, and someone who works directly with congregations, I have seen firsthand the power of feelings in relationships, individuals, and groups. For example, I once knew a talented and gifted pianist who refused to play piano because she felt she wasn't good enough, despite the fact that her skill level was much higher than most. Marriages can crumble because one person feels insecure, which gets reflected in their attitude and breaks up the marriage. I have seen people work extra hard to have friends only to drive away the very same people they wanted to be with.

I don't want anyone to think I flippantly reject feelings as immature or nonexistent. They are powerful and real and can cause many problems when left unsupervised. Feelings have the power to affect our emotional state.

SHAPE YOUR EMOTIONS

Let me say that feelings are to be shaped. We shape our feelings to line up with the kind of life we want. This frustrated world is attempting to conclude for us that feelings are king. Advertisers try to make us feel inadequate with where we are in life and what we have. The media challenges us to imagine what could have been or should have been. This is extremely damaging, because it causes a person's bad feelings to become their reality, even affecting their natural biology. I have seen cases where feelings even take precedence over facts. People determine certain outcomes even though the truth doesn't add up. They believe that the way they feel about something is the way it is, period.

From a Christian perspective, I can clearly see examples of this in the Bible. In one account, a man named Gideon said of himself, *"Look at me. My clan's the weakest in Manasseh and I'm the runt of the litter"* (Judges 16:15, MSG). This man was afraid. In fact, he was hiding in the night, threshing out grain for bread so the neighboring enemies wouldn't see him. Yet God didn't agree with his feelings. With the help of God, Gideon changed—or rather, we could say that he reshaped his emotional state. After changing his thinking about himself, he led an army of three hundred to defeat an enemy of thousands.

Another great example was King Saul. When people hear of Saul, they recognize him as the first king of Israel. Most people think he was always a man of confidence, on top of his game, ready for whatever came his way. After all, how can you be a king of a nation without such self-confidence?

Truth be told, before he became king of Israel, he had a bad image of himself. Saul said, *"But I'm only a Benjaminite, from the smallest of Israel's tribes, and from the most insignificant clan in the tribe at that. Why are you talking to me like this?"* (1 Samuel 9:21, MSG) According to his feelings, he was insignificant and irrelevant. He had to change this wrong perspective to recover from his feelings of inadequacy.

The ability to shape our emotions is the key to reaching the endless possibilities within us.

When you study the lives of accomplished men and women, you'll discover how important it is for us to be able to shape our feelings. Everyone has to face their insecurities head-on and triumph over them to realize their dreams.

Thomas Edison was once told by a teacher that he was too stupid to learn, so he ended up educating himself. He was fired from his first jobs because he was to slow. These events had to have had an effect on him, yet he didn't allow those emotions to slow him down. He went on to produce the lightbulb, the phonograph, the movie camera, and hundreds of other inventions we still use today.

There are far too many people on the other end of this spectrum—those who allow feelings to shape them, who allow bad events to hinder their dreams.

Feelings must not be allowed to control us. Rather, they must be shaped to have as little negative effect on us as possible.

FLIMSY AND FRAIL

I'm not saying that we should never feel anything. God created feelings, and they are needed and valued. However, God intended for us to be in control. Our feelings range from happiness to sadness, from peace to worry and everything in between. Both positive and negative emotions are necessary, and certain undeniable feelings will always follow from events in our lives. But we shouldn't partner with the fragilities of fear, rejection, anxiety, guilt, intimidation, lies, and excuses. They should have little to no power over us.

Everyone will be confronted with inadequate feelings that want to bring them down. This book hasn't been written to help people survive these fragile feelings, but to overcome them.

NO ONE ESCAPES

The mind believes what it can see or feel. In other words, the mind feeds off our feelings and emotions. That is opposite to what is revealed in the Bible. We can see in Scripture that we must first renew or change our thinking, and then our feelings will follow. Everyone can remember growing up with misunderstood feelings, believing it must just be who they are. Change becomes impossible with this way of thinking and will lead to disappointment. People like this end up molding themselves to what other people think they should be rather than changing their thinking and shaping their feelings to be who they know they can be.

I often used to think that I was just unlucky, that I wasn't born with the talents and skills others were, that I wasn't as intelligent or gifted as others, that I had to work hard just to get on an even playing field with others. Of course, over time I realized that this doesn't work. This is the opposite of what the Bible calls the fullness of life. A full life is a place where one can be content with everyone and everything. Each of these seven fragile sentiments are revealed in the Bible as hindrances to the fullness of life.

Jesus said, *"I am come that they might have life, and that they might have it more abundantly"* (John 10:10, KJV). What I clearly see from this passage is that *in* Christ Jesus there is abundant life, which is defined as success. When we overcome fragility, we will ultimately have a successful and superior life. Not superior as in "I'm better than you," but superior in terms of quality and performance.

Everyone is looking for this abundant life. This life will come when we overcome the waves of negative emotional feelings inundating us.

Fear is your mind telling you that failure is just ahead.

CHAPTER ONE
Fear

*For you did not receive the spirit of bondage
again to fear, but you received the Spirit of
adoption by whom we cry out, "Abba, Father."*
(Romans 8:15, NKJV)

LET ME BEGIN BY SAYING THAT THIS BOOK WILL NOT LOOK AT all aspects of fear, as defined by etymologists. Webster's has defined fear as "reverence; respect; due regard for rightful authority."[1] In this context, we're looking at the fear of a circumstance, the fear of the Lord, and reverential fear.

THE FEAR OF THE CIRCUMSTANCE
The fear (respect) we feel from standing too close to the edge of a cliff, or sticking our hand into an alligator's mouth, is a good thing. Deciding not to walk out onto a freeway with speeding traffic is a good thing. We have

---

[1] *Webster's New Twentieth Century Dictionary of the English Language*, "Fear." Edited by Harold Whitehall (New York, NY: Publishers Guild, 1949).

respect for dangerous places and situations. These are safeguards God put within us to preserve our lives.

THE FEAR OF THE LORD

It's also necessary to have a fear (respect) of the Lord. When we acknowledge that He is the Creator of all things, including us, that demands a level of fear. If God created the universe and every living thing in the universe, surely He also has the power to dismantle it all.

Fear of God is, very simply, wisdom. One Bible author explains it this way: *"Let all the earth fear the Lord; let all the inhabitants of the world stand in awe of Him"* (Psalms 33:8). Any doctor, scientist, or rationale person can see that we are perfectly put together. The facts of our complex and intricate construction are too great to ignore or brush off as evolution. It is impossible for evolutionists to convince any judicious person that we accidently came to be. The only possible designer is God.

Considering that we are so perfectly put together, how much greater is the Creator than the creation?

REVERENCE

Fear is also defined as reverence. Understanding that God is holy, and that everything about Him is perfect, requires a reverence that only He deserves. When we feel thankful toward God, that is reverence. When we give God the key place in our hearts, that is reverence. When we give God the glory, that is reverence. Again, the Bible calls this wisdom.

Accepting God as our Creator and seeing Him as all-knowing is the beginning of intelligence. Solomon, who was the richest man and possessed everything available in life at his time (including power, fame, and wisdom), ended up writing, *"The fear of the Lord is the beginning of knowledge, but fools despise wisdom and instruction"* (Proverbs 1:7).

Going back to the Webster's definition, you could define fear as respect, reverence, or a due regard for authority. However, this chapter is not about those kinds of fear. This chapter is about something more personal. It's about those fears that produce obstacles and barriers to effectively hinder us from achieving our destinies and delaying our plans. These are the fears that hold us back from becoming what is really in our hearts.

THE SPIRIT OF FEAR

There is such a thing as a spirit of fear.

Perhaps you could have been a professional athlete, but a fear of rejection held you back. Perhaps you could have done that job as well as anyone, but a fear of failure kept you from even applying. Perhaps you could have delivered that speech and run for mayor, but a fear of man stopped you.

> There is such a thing as a spirit of fear.

Fear of failure, rejection, retribution, and embarrassment holds us back. These fears control our reactions and stop talented and gifted people from

3

pursuing their desires. These are fears that obstruct our dreams, and they can even cause mental and intellectual deficiencies.

If not overcome, these fears become a way of life. They unexpectedly control our decisions. They are best described as a spirit of fear. Paul warned Timothy about this, saying, *"For God has not given us a spirit of fear, but of power and of love and of a sound mind"* (2 Timothy 1:7).

A spirit of fear can take hold and influence our choices in life. If not recognized, then facing these fears can affect our physical abilities and mental states.

SIGNPOSTS

Everyone needs to recognize the characteristics and influences of fear in their lives. Some signposts along the way include: a people-pleasing attitude, an inability to say no, disassociating from certain people, and refusing to participate in activities.

People can develop a mentality of failure. They fail to see promotion and change because they're protecting themselves. The spirit of fear also has the power to restrict our ability to love. It distresses a healthy mind.

These characteristics obstruct opportunities and impede us from taking the steps required to change our futures.

When the Bible calls something a spirit, it refers to an influence that occupies a hidden place of power over us. Others might not see it or know it exists. However, thoughts of the fear cause us to recoil and look for a way out. These fears are self-generated. People believe lies about themselves, and those lies are given a superior position in everyday life.

MY FEAR MADE VISIBLE

I once came to the realization that fear played a part in all my insecurities. I had begun to think that this fear dictated who I was, that I couldn't change. I had what Solomon called a fear of man: *"The fear of man brings a snare, but whoever trusts in the Lord shall be safe"* (Proverbs 29:25).

I was afraid of what people thought of me, whether they liked me or not. Were my achievements acceptable? Did I look foolish to them? Did I conduct myself to their liking? These questioned controlled me. On the outside I looked smooth, composed, and unruffled, as long as I could control the environment around me. If I couldn't, if I was expected to do something that made me fearful, such as public speaking, I always had a reason to get out of it.

People become masters at controlling their situations so the fear doesn't get exposed.

Of all the fragile identities in this book, fear was the most prominent in my life. It was my greatest enemy. I had allowed it to take hold and put down roots. Almost everything I did in life was manipulated to accommodate my fear.

RULED BY FEAR

Fear is directly connected to people's opinion of themselves.

If you do an online search for "number one fear," the first page will primarily contain results about the fear of public speaking. This fear had become well-established in my life over a thirty-year period.

I uncovered this fear in a most extreme way when I decided to pursue a change in life. I had an inward sense that I should be a teacher of the Bible. I believed this desire was connected to my destiny.

At the age of thirty-five, I had an opportunity to speak publically at an evening church meeting. The little country church had twelve members that night and I had prepared for two weeks. My stomach was in knots. Feeling light-headed, thoughts of failure and humiliation ran rampant in my mind.

Throughout the worship service, I repeated to myself the words of 2 Timothy 1:7: *"For God has not given us a spirit of fear, but of power and of love and of a sound mind"* (2 Timothy 1:7). I must have repeated this in excess of twenty-five times.

When I got up on the little stage to preach, I was glad that the pulpit was made of solid wood. Hidden behind the pulpit, my left leg and knee shook uncontrollably. I had to concentrate on making sure the other one didn't start to shake too.

When I looked out over the church, my mind went blank and I couldn't remember anything that I had prepared. I read my entire sermon, glad that I had written it down in detail. I thought I had enough material, but instead I finished in about fifteen minutes.

Something prevented me from having the freedom to speak in front of people.

If I wanted to fulfill my inward leading to teach the Bible, I would have to defeat fear. I began to take opportunities to speak publically. I said to myself, *I will do my best. I will prepare and be ready to speak. Only by the help of God will I succeed.*

This was but a small starting place in defeating this seemingly ever-present spirit of fear.

Because I was a Christian, I began to understand that this fear wasn't inside of me. It was attacking my thinking from the outside, controlling my feelings and emotions. Instead of peace and self-confidence, I had extreme fear.

Sometimes we think that we can change overnight. Somehow we will just pray to God and the next day discover that we are changed. Well, I have yet to meet anyone who overcame their fear overnight.

I worked on my fear of man for many years and have finally been set free. I simply try my best, and the fear does not control me any longer. If I falter while speaking and I feel like I could have done better, I just let myself know that I will do better next time.

When we pay less attention to what others think of us, we are set free. This freedom produces the best results and causes us to be the people we were created to be.

SIMPLE YET POWERFUL

Fear begins to take root in our lives in simple ways. We can all remember difficult or bad things that happened to us and affected our self-esteem, usually early in life when we're the most vulnerable. In every capacity, from homes to playgrounds and schools to churches, it seems that our enemy, satan, is trying to plant fear in our lives from an early age.

Fear can also come from people. Today we have experts in fear, people who have bought into the lie of fear-based communication for one purpose: profit. Fear-based media, politicians, and the person next door can all contribute to fears in our thinking.

Fear can also develop from the expectations placed on us by family, friends, employers, and even strangers. These expectations can come from both well-meaning people and not-so-well-meaning people.

People seem to judge us by our ability to make them look good. They expect us to operate at a high level of success, pushing us into a corner when we don't have the talent or gifting required to accomplish their expectations. We often aren't properly trained in how to handle these pressures.

Many times what people expect of us isn't what we have in our hearts to do. Over time we begin to believe others and view our fears as a necessary protection from danger. *I have to be careful,* we think, *or I could be eliminated.*

It seems today that people are almost drawn to fear. So many people struggle with fear in their emotional health.

FEAR EXPOSED

Of course, fear doesn't go hand in hand with a peaceful life. Fear doesn't only agitate us; it ends up being a torment, causing us to have an unhealthy frame of mind. John explained that fear is unnatural:

There is no fear in love; but perfect love casts out fear, because fear involves torment. *But he who fears has not been made perfect in love.* (1 John 4:18, emphasis added)

We know that God is love. As John says, there is no fear in love. In other words, God is fearless. Fear involves torment, God does not torment people. He is love. This proves that fear is unnatural to us and needs to be replaced in our lives. Fear will produce faithless actions, but peace will produce faith-filled actions.

FEAR CONQUERED

How do we know that fear has been conquered? Mark wrote,

But He was in the stern, asleep on a pillow. And they awoke Him and said to Him, "Teacher, do You not care that we are perishing?"

Then He arose and rebuked the wind, and said to the sea, "Peace, be still!" And the wind ceased and there was a great calm. But He said to them, "Why are you so fearful? How is it that you have no faith?" (Mark 4:38–40)

Imagine the fear and turmoil going on in everyone's mind. Imagine every wave coming up over the side of the boat in an attempt to sink it. The disciples had to hold on to whatever was nearest just to keep from being thrown overboard. The wind drove rain relentlessly into their faces, making it impossible to see. Fear was mounting and hope fading fast. The only possible solution they could see was Jesus, asleep on a pillow in the back of the boat.

Could this be a clue to fearless faith? Imagine Jesus as He gets up and roars, "Peace, be still!" All of a sudden the boat was floating in perfectly calm waters. No wind, no waves, no rain. The Bible says it was a great calm. Everything was still. The disciples would have looked over the lake and saw nothing but clear, glasslike water. Only the insignificant sound of water lightly splashing against the side of the boat.

Was Jesus demonstrating an important life lesson here? Fear produces no faith, and that will sink your boat. However, peace produces great faith, which calms the situation and takes you to the other side.

Even though the fear of sinking was all around Him, Jesus slept. The peace Jesus had ended up producing a calm, protected, and satisfied trip. Jesus summed up the truth by asking, *"Where is your faith?"* (Luke 8:25)

When you have peace in a situation, you know you have overcome fear. Overcoming fear isn't a matter of prayer. Prayer is important, and we should pray, especially for peace, but it's only one part of conquering our fears. Jesus said twelve times in the Bible, either to His disciples or other people, "Do not fear" or "Why are you so fearful?" If people had no authority over their fear, Jesus would be unjust in questioning them. If all they had to do was pray or get someone else to pray, Jesus would have told them so.

The process of eliminating fear comes in phases as we move from fear to peace.

A PARTIAL VICTORY

Episodes in our lives can uncover incomplete healing. The fear we thought was eradicated rears its ugly head and we realize there is still some residue left. There will be times when we think we have overcome a fear, but at other times we'll realize that the fear is still there. These are partial or incomplete victories over fear. A partial victory does not assure triumph over fear.

In the Bible, there is a story where Peter walks on water for a short way. He had been with Jesus for many years and seen some amazing miracles. Together they had overcome some fearful events. Peter thought he was fearless because of his past victories with Jesus.

This account details the power of fear and shows that fear can be more powerful than even God's desire for you to accomplish great things. Even though Jesus called Peter to walk on the water, and obviously Peter wanted to because he got out of the boat, his fear obstructed the plan. It was only a partial victory.

Operating in fear can become second nature to us, and we don't even realize its presence. However, there will always come a time when our fears are exposed, like with Peter.

I particularly like the facts as presented by Matthew:

So He said, "Come." And when Peter had come down out of the boat, he walked on the water to go to Jesus. But when he saw that the wind was boisterous, he was afraid; and beginning to sink he cried out, saying, "Lord, save me!"

And immediately Jesus stretched out His hand and caught him, and said to him, "O you of little faith, why did you doubt?" (Matthew 14:29–31)

Notice that Jesus addressed the fear. It seems almost foolish. Should not Peter be congratulated for attempting this adventure, considering that the other disciples stayed in the boat? Yet Jesus didn't acknowledge Peter's brave attempt at walking on water by faith. Evidently it was far more important to address his fear, a fear which would have to be faced again in the near future.

Fear affects Peter again during the time of Jesus' crucifixion, when Peter denied knowing Him. If his fear hadn't been addressed, Peter would not have fulfilled his purpose. His purpose was not to walk on water; his purpose was to continue on after Jesus' crucifixion, taking the same message of salvation to the people. This would require fearless courage.

No matter how vital or ordinary our purpose is, fear can affect the result. When we desire to do something exciting or new or innovative, our fear can be more powerful than our desire. That's why overcoming fear is vital to success in life. It doesn't matter how old you are

> **When Jesus brings something up, it's more than just information. It's transformation!**

or what you have accomplished; fear can still hinder you.

Jesus confronted fear regularly. He warned us that fear has consequences and we should be cautious of its power. When Jesus brings something up, it's more than just information. It's transformation!

John enlightens us, *"This is the message which we have heard from Him and declare to you, that God is light and in Him is <u>no darkness at all</u>"* (1 John 1:5, emphasis added).

When Jesus exposes darkness, there is always a way out of its grip. Bible teachings give us the authority to transform the areas in our lives that have been exposed. Begin to take your place of victory. Step into what God has for you by overcoming the grip of fear.

THE FEAR OF THE FIRST STEP

Before I could speak comfortably to large groups, I had to be able to speak comfortably to ten or twenty people. I took many important little steps: saying a prayer in public over a meal, thanking someone publically, or making an announcement at church. All were opportunities to conquer my fear. Before I could teach a Bible school course, God allowed me to teach a small Bible study. These steps take time, each one conquering a little territory that fear once held.

The first step is the most difficult. This is when fear is the fiercest. It just seems easier to not try at all. Every possible reason to give up will expose itself. The first step will always seem fearful until you conquer it.

LEARNING TO SWIM

A good example of overcoming fear is my experience of teaching myself to swim. When I grew up, we didn't have swimming lessons or a pool big enough to swim in. We had a river close by, though: the Assiniboine River. Our swimming lessons took place down at the river, with no lifeguard and no supervision.

The river wasn't large, but it did have a decent current, especially in the springtime. If I wanted to be able to run into the river like the big kids, no holds barred, I had to overcome my fear of the first step. What was in the river that I didn't know about? How big were the fish? Did fish bite? What about those little crayfish... would they come after me? How far would I have to go into the river before the bottom dropped off? Two steps? Five steps? Would that current overpower me and sweep me downstream, never to be heard of again?

Fear will create a whole metropolis of questions, and of course some are valid. If I ran full-tilt into the river the first time, I could very well have been swept away.

Everyone should start overcoming fears on their tiptoes. Just like with swimming, you're testing the waters. The next day, you go a little farther—but not past the waist. You can still see the bottom. No animals, no surprises. You try swimming at that level, which isn't as much fun but it's a good place to learn.

Taking the first step has a lot to do with overcoming your fear of the unknown. Start out slow and discover the unknown; it's usually not as fearful as you first think.

As a kid, just before I fell asleep at night, I would think about going back to the river to try again. As I drifted off, I knew I was going to go deeper the next day. I would know a little more. The animals didn't bite and the river bottom was as firm as packed sand. I would push a little farther, one step at a time.

In the days that followed, I got neck-deep in the river.

I needed to be careful at this stage, so this is where I spent the most time perfecting my swimming skills. I may not have completely overcome my fear, but it felt pretty good. I was getting better and it seemed to me that most kids didn't go much deeper anyway—except, of course, the really good swimmers.

We need to be careful not to stop at this phase, thinking it's good enough. This only reveals that we're still limited by fear, that it still hasn't been completely eradicated in your lives.

At the next level, I waded out on my tiptoes, bouncing up and down as I gently felt the current pulling me—but not too far. I swam back towards shore.

I began dreaming of crossing to the other side. One day, I went for it, never looking up, just kicking and stroking as hard as I could. I stood in two feet of water on the other side, amazed at the how easy it had been.

In time, I started running down into the river without fear.

By overcoming the fear of swimming in the river, I soon got to swim in a lake, and even in the ocean. Eventually it was possible for me to jump into a pool from a thirty-foot platform. I could fearlessly ride on boats too.

Conquering any fear is no different than when I was ten years old learning to swim. You have to keep going until you conquer its effects. Once you conquer the fear, you'll wonder what all the hullabaloo was about.

Today it seems almost foolish that I once allowed any space in my life for the fear of man. The fear is but a faded memory of an enemy that once seemed so powerful. When you know that overcoming the thing you fear is not only possible, but with the help of God easier than you thought, you'll experience the most freedom you will ever feel.

Rejection is your mind telling you that you are unloved.

CHAPTER TWO
Rejection

Even if my father and mother should desert me,
you will take care of me.
(Psalms 27:10, CEV)

REJECTION IS WHEN YOU FEEL UNACCEPTABLE, FAULTY, OR useless. It's one of the most deeply hurtful emotions anyone can experience. Every one of us, from the most powerful to the most vulnerable has, experienced rejection. There are no exceptions.

Rejection has undeniable characteristics, but the bottom line is that it hurts. People with extreme rejection issues feel like they have no value or are unwanted. It can be felt in life in a couple of ways.

First, people reject us. This can include anyone from a sibling to an enemy, from a close companion to a complete stranger. Rejection can be experienced in any area of life, including the places where you think you should be the safest, like at work, with your family, or even at church. And it usually happens for no apparent reason that we can determine.

Secondly, we reject ourselves. We can create rejection in our lives through wrong thinking, making us feel unacceptable even to ourselves. In addition to us thinking we're undesirable, this kind of rejection produces words, actions, and attitudes that cause others to reject us in turn. We end up in a cycle of not wanting to be rejected, but causing our own rejection through defense mechanisms.

It doesn't matter whether people reject us or we reject ourselves, it all comes down to expectations.

UNREALISTIC BELIEFS

Expectations are placed on us from holding impractical beliefs. These beliefs are created in the mind and come from our own idealism. At times, the expectations we place on ourselves are naïve and unrealistic. We've all watched talent shows where contestants believe they are professionals, but the rest of us can easily see they aren't.

On the other hand, unrealistic ideas can be placed on us by others. Many times these are impossible for us to meet, and we feel rejected because we cannot live up to their standard.

WHEN DOES REJECTION START?

Rejection starts early in life—so early that many of us cannot even remember the first time we felt it. But if you look back, you may find that your strongest memories include feelings of rejection. These may be times when we were ridiculed by our peers for something we said or did. We buckled up our boots and decided to do better next time to be more acceptable.

Rejection could go back to a father who was distant and cold. Maybe he always seemed too busy for you. Maybe you didn't think you were good enough for your mother or father. Maybe it seemed like your parents had favorites. Did they seem to pay more attention to a sibling? Maybe you weren't popular in high school or no one ever asked you out on a date.

Did you date someone for years only to have them leave you? Did your husband or wife leave you for someone else? Were you not recognized for a promotion or get the same benefits as others? Did you feel rejected by your children when they grew up and hardly ever came to see you? The possibilities are endless.

Without knowing it, we often decide that we need to perform better to be recognized. We think, *I will be accepted, no matter how hard I have to work at this. In fact, if I have to reject someone else to be acceptable myself, then so be it.* This tactic will create more rejection further down the road of life. We then become the rejecters, the dreaded enemy we don't want to face ourselves.

REJECTION: LIKE A WOUND

I said in the first chapter that fear can become a spirit. Rejection is more like a wound, or a deep emotional pain.

Some people learn to live with the pain, believing they are functioning normally. Even though the wound flares up every once in a while, they have coping mechanisms in place to deal with it. For others, the wound can fester and affect their very survival.

No matter if we are good at hiding rejection or terrible at it, rejection problems will put your life on hold. The low self-esteem that rejection produces will steal someone's very purpose in life.

Many people cannot transact with their family, work, or interests because rejection has taken a top spot on their list of priorities. Feelings of rejection can turn into a wound that opens easily or even stays open permanently. You can go through life for days, or even weeks, without any trouble, but then someone says something or does something, and the wound is open again.

This wound can drive people into sadness and depression. Just like when someone doesn't take care of a physical wound, it can become infected. In the case of rejection, the wound tells us what to do. We learn what opens the wound. We learn to stay away from people and places. People with rejection begin to hide, thinking no one cares about them. Why should they have to deal with those hurtful feelings when they can just stay by themselves and be okay? The results of this tactic are truly damaging. We were created for relationship, and without relationship we begin to wither.

MARKS OF REJECTION

The fallout of rejection can be far-ranging, and people who fight rejection can begin to think that life is unfair and they have been short-changed. They imagine that others don't have to go through what they have to. When you have these deep-seated feelings of rejection, it only takes a memory or triggering incident for the hurt to be felt all over again.

Some reactions may not be easily seen at first, like isolation. Isolation is when someone becomes unsocial and unavailable. Another reaction is to become manipulative and attempt to receive praise from others. Others become frosty or defensive towards people who may just want to help. Here is a reaction that's especially damaging: people can become people-pleasers, doing anything to avoid feelings of rejection. Finally, those who cannot handle rejection can become rebellious in their attitude and unable to receive correction.

The products of rejection are far-ranging and difficult to pinpoint. It can be anything from anger to hopelessness. We see rejection as the cause of inferiority and defensiveness. Envy, rebellion, and resentment can all be effects of rejection.

However, it doesn't have to be this way.

NOT ABSOLUTE

In fact, the gospels reveal that rejection never affected Jesus. The rejection Jesus went through got Him crucified, but when He went to the cross He had victory, not rejection, on His mind. John said, *"He came to his own people, but they didn't want him"* (John 1:11, MSG). Luke reveals that Jesus said, *"Father, forgive them; they don't know what they're doing"* (Luke 23:34, MSG).

> **When we feel rejected but have a good understanding of our own worth, rejection loses its strength.**

This shows that there is power in living above rejection. When we feel rejected but have a good understanding of our own worth, rejection loses its strength.

A BETTER WAY

There is an account of twelve brothers who lived four thousand years ago during the reign of Pharaohs Senusret II and Senusret III of Egypt's Twelfth Dynasty. Through these brothers, we can see both the harmful and triumphant effects of rejection.

One brother seemed to be accepted by their father above the others, so one day the others decided to do something about it.

When Joseph came up to his brothers, they ripped off his long robe with full sleeves. Then they took him and threw him into the well, which was dry.

While they were eating, they suddenly saw a group of Ishmaelites traveling from Gilead to Egypt. Their camels were loaded with spices and resins. Judah said to his brothers, "What will we gain by killing our brother and covering up the murder? Let's sell him to these Ishmaelites. Then we won't have to hurt him; after all, he is our brother, our own flesh and blood." His brothers agreed, and when some Midianite traders came by, the brothers pulled Joseph out of the well and sold him for twenty pieces of silver to the Ishmaelites, who took him to Egypt. (Genesis 37:23–28, GNT)

Feelings of rejection drove this family into chaos, but Joseph, the brother who was sold, didn't allow his family's rejection to destroy his life. It took about twenty years to reconcile the damage, but in the end the family came back together, living in harmony and unity. You can read the whole account starting in Genesis 37, how Joseph reacted to his brothers' rejection and ended up providing healing for the entire family. However, two scriptures towards the end of this account sum up Joseph's attitude towards his brothers' rejection:

And Joseph said to his brothers, "Please come near to me." So they came near. Then he said: "I am Joseph your brother, whom you sold into Egypt. But now, do not therefore be grieved or angry with yourselves because you sold me here; for God sent me before you to preserve life. (Genesis 45:4–5, NKJV)

It all boils down to how we handle the adversity of rejection.

AN EPISODE TO REMEMBER

During my early years in ministry, I came to know a young man who overcame rejection in a big way. After knowing this man for a few years, he told me his extraordinary story. He was from India, and had become a Christian. Outraged, his father and brothers locked him in a small building along the river where they lived. He was told that their plan was to sacrifice him to the river gods in the morning.

As he knelt on the floor, his face to the ground in prayer, he heard the words "Get up and flee from here." He looked up and found the door to the small building open. He got up and ran from his family, never looking back.

He never contacted his family again, for fear of reprisal.

Over the years, in India, he educated himself in university, married, and had a baby girl. It was during this time that I received his application to attend Bible school in Canada. We get numerous applications from people overseas and I didn't know his story, but I felt compelled to pursue his application.

In the years since his acceptance into Bible school, he has managed to bring his wife and child to Canada. His mother-in-law, too, has been accepted to live in Canada. He has finished his doctorate in psychology and is helping many people with emotional problems.

The last time I had contact with him, he was attempting to reconcile with his parents and brothers. He forgave them and wanted to go back to India and visit them.

These are big victories over rejection. Sometimes we think our rejection is more severe than others. I'm comfortable in saying that our rejection is often a small matter compared to others. No matter the level of rejection we face, victory is in our own hands. How we handle rejection will determine whether we're powerful or powerless.

ONE EXPERIENCE

We all have an inward view and think about ourselves in a certain way. No one else knows for sure how we see ourselves. I can make it through life unscathed from rejection if I'm the only one who knows my defaults.

Some incidents of rejection seem to stick more than others. They seem to be more powerful than the usual cases, like not getting chosen for a sports team or being labeled for something we said or did.

After one particular event in my life, I became determined to never again put myself in a similar predicament ever again. My school put on a drama performance every year that included both high school and elementary students, each having a part to play. A call went out for anyone interested in being part of the drama team that year. As long as you came to the initial meeting, you would be allowed to perform.

I was given a one-line part in a short skit. I thought my line could be funnier than it was, so I elaborated on it a little during practice. To my surprise, the drama teacher walked up to me, in front of everyone, bent me over, and spanked my behind. There were about thirty to forty kids there, including all the older kids up to Grade Twelve.

I was completely embarrassed.

The teacher then explained to me that my part would be just a walk-up, that I would just pretend to whisper my line into my co-actor's ear.

On the night of the performance, everyone still laughed and got the joke, but I didn't again volunteer to do anything in front of the public. I attempted every means possible to avoid being up in front of people. My self-esteem had been tested and I'd failed. My inability to handle rejection ended up contributing to the spirit of fear I spoke about in Chapter One.

CONFIDENCE

It's vital to understand that rejection can cause people to have poor self-esteem. Self-esteem means having a good opinion of oneself. People with good self-esteem have a balanced estimation of themselves. They have a positive attitude, judgment, and outlook. They understand what is attainable.

If we're not careful with rejection, we can develop a poor opinion of ourselves. This opinion will affect every area of our lives. It has been shown that a poor self-image is the number one factor in limiting a person's potential achievements.

When we're young, we don't know that we have limits. We think the sky is the limit when it comes to our talent. We think we can be good at everything, and we want to try everything. That's exactly the way it's supposed to be.

Everybody needs to discover who they are young in life. These early experiences support a person's path to finding their destiny.

However, if you're never taught how to handle rejection, your life will always revolve around being acceptable to your peers and the people you look up to. If parents fail to coach and prepare their children in their talents and giftings, the children will suffer.

We must all understand that no one is great at everything. Everybody has limits in some areas and are limitless in others. When we find our God-given capacities, the possibilities are boundless.

THE REAL MEDALISTS

In life, we seem to acknowledge and accept the victors. We celebrate and recognize their accomplishments, but we seldom remember the people who came in second, third, fourth, and on down the list. If they're not careful, second-place finishers can allow feelings of rejection to eat away at their core. They may fail to see that they're just as valuable as the victors.

The victors have accomplished a temporary goal. In the grand scheme of things, their accomplishments are but a fading memory. Can anyone tell me who the greatest gladiator who ever lived was? How many battles did he win? Or who won the Olympic gold medal for the men's one-hundred-meter race in 1928? Who is the greatest hockey player to ever live? (This is yet to be determined, and ever will be!)

If you want to compete for a gold medal, be a hockey player or become a gladiator, by all means. Go for it. But don't base your worth and acceptance on it. We all want to be winners, but the facts tell us that only one in approximately twenty-five million people will win an Olympic gold medal in their lifetime. It's impossible to measure yourself by these standards.

The real medalists are the one who continue to live life to the fullest. They may have not been recognized, or even thanked, but they're still the people God created them to be.

IS IT INEVITABLE?

The greatest advantage in overcoming rejection is to know that rejection is inevitable. In other words, we are incapable of avoiding rejection. There is no way of living on this earth without being rejected from time to time. When we accept that rejection is part of life, it begins to lose it power over us.

No matter how much rejection you experience in life there is a right way and a wrong way to view it. The right view changes your attitude about yourself, which destroys rejection's strength.

You're not unusual if you feel rejection. It doesn't matter whether you're a Christian, atheist, or agnostic, you will face rejection for what and how you believe. See, God created us for relationship, so rejection isn't natural for us. We were created first and foremost for relationship with God, and then relationship with others.

> *What then shall we say to these things? If God is for us, who can be against us?"* (Romans 8:31)

People will reject us, but our Heavenly Father never does or never will. If we keep this in proper perspective, we will see rejection for what it really is: an irritation. Jesus confirmed that He felt rejection, but that the rejection had no power. He explains that anyone who decides to become a Christian will feel the pains of rejection just as He did.

> *A disciple is not above his teacher, nor a servant above his master.* (Matthew 10:24)

In other words, the rejection Jesus endured will be felt by believers, only to a lesser degree.

The sooner we accept that rejection is real and unavoidable, the sooner we will get on with living in freedom. This doesn't mean that we just trample on people and tell them we don't care what they think. No, we recognize their feelings of rejection and understand that we shouldn't brush off others who project it. Understanding that others struggle with rejection, and try with all their might to avoid being rejected, helps with our own sense of rejection when someone pushes back at us. We need to accept them and realize that they're under the power of rejection, knowing that they will, from time to time, turn their rejection on us, no matter how close we are.

Even if you've been married fifty years, your spouse can still communicate rejection every once in a while. There will be plenty of times and plenty of ways to experience the sting of rejection.

ACCIDENTAL

Another great help in overcoming rejection is knowing that people often reject us without knowing it. Everyone is looking after themselves and trying to be accepted. Interestingly, this God-given desire for acceptance seems to cause people to project rejection. People do this by refusing to acknowledge or encourage our efforts. No matter how hard someone tries to support you, they can and will fail you. Everyone must understand this natural side effect of being human.

Some parents are unaware and oblivious to the hurt of their child. A best friend might walk away from the friendship for no good reason. A spouse may push their partner away, never knowing the other feels the same rejection. Even God gets rejected for not answering a person's prayer the way they thought He should.

Without knowing it, the initial wounds of rejection sometimes become unrecognizable over the years and people just live with them.

BE GOOD WITH YOURSELF

What everyone needs to see is that rejection doesn't have to be fatal. Isaiah, speaking about Jesus, has given rejection one of its fullest definitions.

He was looked down on and passed over, a man who suffered, who knew pain firsthand. One look at him and people turned away. We looked down on him, thought he was scum. (Isaiah 53:3, MSG)

What we know about Jesus is that He overcame these influences of rejection. He went on to fulfill His life's purpose. Jesus didn't look at rejection as a problem that needed to be conquered. He looked at Himself

> **Rejection can be recognized and then disallowed.**
> **In other words, rejection can be rejected.**

and accepted His mission and purpose. In others words, He was good with who He was. He was good with how God had made Him.

Jesus' attitude should be our attitude. He is one of the best living examples of limiting rejection's influence. Rejection can be recognized and then disallowed.

In other words, rejection can be rejected.

Anxiety is your mind telling you that an outcome is unsure.

CHAPTER THREE
Anxiety

Peace I leave with you, My peace I give to you;
not as the world gives do I give to you. Let not
your heart be troubled, neither let it be afraid.
(John 14:27)

YOU WILL FIND THAT THERE ARE VARIOUS DEFINITIONS for anxiety, depending on your area of expertise. In medicine, you might define anxiety differently than psychology. Those in social and rehabilitation work define anxiety differently than theologians.

Webster's defines anxiety as "concern or solitude respecting some event, future or uncertain, which disturbs the mind and keeps it in a sense of painful uneasiness."[2] Elsewhere, it's defined as "a feeling of worry, nervousness, or unease, typically about an imminent event or something with an uncertain outcome."[3]

---

[2] Ibid., "Anxiety."

[3] *Heal Your Life*, "Anxiety." Date of access: August 25, 2017 (https://www.healyourlife.com/sub-topic/anxiety).

I like to define anxiety for what it's called in the Bible: worry. We become worried because we don't know the outcome of something that could take place later in life.

You may have grown accustomed to being full of anxiety without really knowing it. As a created person, we are able to convince ourselves to adapt and attune our lives around phenomena such as anxiety. These worries and fears prevent us from living our life the way God intended. Anxiety can blind the mind and become a weight that affects our freedom.

The root of deeper emotional problems is almost always anxiety. We need to constantly keep our foot on the neck of anxiety because it will lead to complications in our emotional, physical, and spiritual health.

Like a doorway, people worry themselves into agitation, dread, and even anxiety attacks. These are the building blocks of depression. A depressed person is always a worried person.

DEPRESSION

Today's understanding of depression is limited. Some suggest that depression is a chemical imbalance in the brain. Others suggest that depression is a malfunction of the network of cells in the brain that connects to our emotions. The Bible reveals that anxiety is a result of running our own lives without God. Without the principles and trust God asks of us, life can become overwhelming.

There is plenty of evidence that depression has a multitude of physical side effects. We see people with stomach problems, headaches, chest pain, sleep disorders, and weight gain, to name a few. These aren't just side effects of depression, but also of anxiety and worry.

Some people think that depression is somehow genetic or innate (something that was in one at birth), but all depressives come from a background of pain and dread. If you assess the early patterns of depressives, you'll see that the catalyst is anxiety. If anxiety is allowed to flourish, the fruit of it is depression.

I cannot speak to the diagnosis of depression because I'm not qualified, other than to say that healing is available. If you suffer from depression, God loves you no differently than any other person on the planet. In fact, healing is always available for everyone. Matthew says that

> *Jesus went around visiting all the towns and villages. He taught in the synagogues, preached the Good News about the Kingdom, and healed people with* every kind *of disease and sickness.* (Matthew 9:35, GNT, emphasis added)

Jesus provided healings for anything that afflicted people, and we can also trust Him with our anxiety. If Jesus did this for one person, we know He will do the same for us.

Jesus Christ is the same yesterday, today, and forever. (Hebrews 13:8)

ENEMIES

From a careful study of Scripture, we can see that anxiety led King David to depression. David, a man after God's own heart, had depressive behaviors that needed healing.

The cause of his depression is described as oppression from his enemies. He believed that people were out to get him.

Whether real or make-believe, many people live under the weight of enemies. Enemies don't have to be a person, or group of persons. Enemies can attack our thinking from all sources. We can have enemies of self-worth and value. We can have enemies of indecision and fear. We can have enemies that seem to want to attack our marriage, our children, or our careers.

The great news is that David was delivered from depression. Many of the victory psalms were written by him after his period of depression. Let me provide one example, the very last psalm David wrote. I especially like the fourteenth verse, where the words "bowed down" are interpreted as those who are ready to quit.

The Lord helps the fallen and lifts those bent beneath their loads. (Psalms 145:14, NLT)

We can be bent beneath our load by anxiety, but that doesn't mean we have to live under the load. Jesus said,

"For My yoke is easy and My burden is light" (Matthew 11:30).

LEARN TO LIVE IN THE NOW

We need to give ourselves to what we're doing at the moment. I remember where I was when I got a good grasp of the extent of my anxiety. It was Monday, and I was getting ready to go on a four-day fishing trip to Idaho. I was tying my fishing lines and putting everything together for the trip when I realized I was anxious. I was excited about the trip but anxious about what I would need to do when I got back on Friday.

How foolish it was to lose the enjoyment of that trip to anxiety. I realized that I had to make a conscious effort to stop stewing. I should have been thinking about fishing, the scenery, and the good company I would have, contemplating the refreshing outdoors and the possibility of catching a big fish. Instead I was already dreading the day I got back, worried about how far behind I would be.

Other words for anxiety are dread, fearful expectation, or anticipation. I was dreading coming back to what I had to get done. Again, I didn't know the outcome, but I felt that it might not turn out well.

Without realizing it, my dread caused gloominess to set in, which almost made me want to stay home. Why should I go if I had so many things that needed to be done at home?

As you can see, worry can affect our joy. Worry or dreading things can convince us that the things we like doing are just too much of an inconvenience. The discomfort of worry isn't worth it, so we think it's safer not to do the things we like. An endless cycle of unfulfilled accomplishments can begin to set in. Everyone must realize that it's their choice whether to enjoy something or not.

CONCERN

We all know what concern feels like. Our heart pounds before a big presentation or a tough exam. We get butterflies in our stomach before that speech. We fret over a family problem.

These will come and these will go. In fact, the Bible lets us know that concerns in life will always be around. But we must handle them carefully. The Good News Bible explains it this way: *"Don't worry about anything,*

> Begin to see anxiety as a bother rather than a problem. Realize that anxiety can be taken out of our lives.

but in all your prayers ask God for what you need, always asking him with a thankful heart" (Philippians 4:6, GNT).

Begin to see anxiety as a bother rather than a problem. Realize that anxiety can be taken out of our lives. When you're tempted to worry, challenge it with the Bible truth.

> *Therefore humble yourselves under the mighty hand of God, that He may exalt you in due time, casting all your care upon Him, for He cares for you.* (1 Peter 5:6–7)

Remember, anxiety is a feeling of worry about an upcoming event with an uncertain outcome. If the outcome is uncertain, the worry is premature. Why worry about something that might or might not happen? Whenever we put our trust in God, we can safely say it will turn out good.

ANXIETY HAS NO POWER

When I first read, *"Don't worry about anything, but in all your prayers ask God for what you need, always asking him with a thankful heart"* (Philippians 4:6, GNT), I thought, does that really means everything? In the past I believed that my anxiety helped change my circumstances. If I had concern, then being concerned about the concern would help fix the concern. In other words, if I worried about something, my worry would produce a solution to the problem. It seemed to have worked on a number of occasions.

I remember being anxious that I might not get a certain promotion. I thought about it constantly and even worried that I might not be seen as a viable candidate. I did end up getting that promotion. To me, this was evidence that anxiety worked. After a few of these episodes I began to think that it pays to be anxious— that it pays to worry, to stay up at night thinking every possibility through, whether good or bad. Over time you begin to have more and more things to be anxious about. I began to realize that this worry wasn't compatible with an enjoyable life. A worry-free life was more appealing.

Freedom came when I began trusting God, no matter the outcome. Learning to trust God, I discovered that I could receive answers without needing to be anxious about the problems. I never seemed to take into account the fact that the things I was worried about in the past could work out the same way without the worry. It was like I wanted to play a role in the outcome of a situation that seemed beyond my control.

It feels good to have an outcome better than the one we worried about. However, this is not life's best. When it seems like the predictable outcome might not be good, put your trust in God. He can make it good. Enjoying life's best requires faith and having trust in God that all things will work out for the good.

YOU CHOOSE

Clarity is always the beginning of the healing process, so let's add some clarity to anxiety. Sometimes people think they cannot choose to have peace in their lives because of all the problems they face. They may think that they don't have the ability to choose how they feel. They may believe that their feelings of anxiety have a right to exist, that anxiety is the only option.

Jesus used some words to help us see a truth that seems distant to so many:

Peace I leave with you, My peace I give to you; not as the world gives do I give to you. Let not

your heart be troubled, neither let it be afraid.
(John 14:27)

The word "troubled," meaning to be agitated or stirred, is used to describe what worry is like. Jesus was saying that we shouldn't let our hearts be stirred or agitated. Correspondingly, the words "let not" show that we have a choice in the matter. I will not let my heart be troubled. I have the right to not allow it to be part of me. We choose to either allow ourselves to be stirred or we disallow it.

OUR THOUGHTS PLAY A PART

During His Olivet discourse, Jesus told His listeners all about anxiety:

This is why I tell you: do not be worried about the food and drink you need in order to stay alive, or about clothes for your body. After all, isn't life worth more than food? And isn't the body worth more than clothes? Look at the birds: they do not plant seeds, gather a harvest and put it in barns; yet your Father in heaven takes care of them! Aren't you worth much more than birds? Can any of you live a bit longer by worrying about it?

And why worry about clothes? Look how the wild flowers grow: they do not work or make clothes for themselves. But I tell you that not even King Solomon with all his wealth had clothes as beautiful as one of these flowers. It is God who clothes the wild grass—grass that is here today and gone tomorrow, burned up in the oven. Won't he be all the more sure to clothe you? What little faith you have!

So do not start worrying: "Where will my food come from? or my drink? or my clothes?" (These are the things the pagans are always concerned about.) Your Father in heaven knows that you need all these things. Instead, be concerned above everything else with the Kingdom of God and with what he requires of you, and he will provide you with all these other things. So do not worry about tomorrow; it will have enough worries of its own. There is no need to add to the troubles each day brings. (Matthew 6:25–34, GNT)

Understand our responsibility towards anxiety. One noteworthy truth from this passage is that Jesus said, "Do not be worried." It is our assignment to not be worried. In the King James Version, Jesus used the phrases "take no thought" or "why take thought" five times. Other translations have Jesus telling us to stop worrying about our lives, or to stop being anxious about our lives. He uses the example of the basics of life to expose the struggles of anxiety. He has set into place the principle of overcoming anxiety, and this will translate into every area of our lives where we may have reason to worry.

TAKE THEM OR LEAVE THEM

"Take no thought" implies that thoughts are there for the taking or leaving, as though our thoughts can be laid out on an abstract list. On this list is everything that pertains to life, all the things we may have taught ourselves or been taught by others over time. This list is extensive and includes everything we need for our present circumstances and future possibilities.

A second thing to note from this passage is that it points towards the fact that *all* thoughts are for our taking to rejecting. Jesus doesn't give us any other alternative to handling our thoughts. He simply said, "Don't take the ones that are anxious." Of course, we've seen in an earlier scripture that prayer is always available. Through a combination of our prayer and our choice, we can reject thoughts of worry.

Everyone has the strength to change the anxieties they face. We will have to make a quality decision when it comes to thoughts of anxiety. Do we take them or refuse them? In fact, we are making choices in so many areas of our lives that we don't even realize that each day we are either taking thought or rejecting thoughts from this list. We are where we are today because we've thought about our choices and made some.

THOUGHTS ALWAYS ARE

The word *thought* means "an idea; a conception of the mind, as a judgment; an opinion; a conclusion... that which springs from, originates in, or is produced by imagination; a creation of the mind having a distinct existence from the mind that created it; a fancy; a conceit; a conception."[4]

We feed our intellect through our eyes and ears. All thought originates from experiences of things we've seen or heard. You may worry about your kids because you saw or heard something they're involved in. You may have anxiety about your job because you heard on the news about a possible recession or a slow economy.

Anxiety flows around the belief that something bad might happen. On the other side, maybe something bad has already happened. Nevertheless, we can refuse to worry.

For example, your spouse may have already left you, but you can become anxious that it will be impossible to make it on your own. You may not have tried or asked God for help yet, but you assume it'll be impossible. A lot of the times anxiety is fantasy from something we perceive could happen because we've heard the possibility exists.

Another example I use is that people live with the anxiety of being attacked by someone and maybe even killed. Statistics show that in Canada you are twenty times more likely to die in a car accident than be killed by a stranger, yet we have no fear of getting into our vehicles and traveling an hour down a freeway to go shopping. The media may overplay the story of the person who was killed by a stranger because it rates well, rather

---

[4] *Webster's New Twentieth Century Dictionary of the English Language*, "Thought." Edited by Harold Whitehall (New York, NY: Publishers Guild, 1949).

than car accidents that happen by the dozen every day. If you were watching car accidents for an hour on the news, you would become afraid of driving. We can either choose thoughts or leave thoughts. The choice is ours.

CONFUSION

Confusion is a result of not trusting in God but rather trying to accomplish or find answers in our own strength. I like how Joyce Meyers phrased it one time. Paraphrased, she said, "The moment I get confused, I've gone too far in my own planning. When I sense frustration and confusion, I've stopped receiving God's grace and gotten into works."

Wanting to understand everything is a problem, because no one can understand everything. Wisdom tells us to plan for tomorrow, and we should, but no one can tell with certainty the details of their future. When we try to figure it out, we can get more bogged down by out cares and concerns. Too much human reasoning, and not enough trusting in the Lord, can lead to more anxiety and fear.

EXCESS REASONING

There is such a thing as excess reasoning. Excessive reasoning is when you take thinking beyond what is needed or

> Excessive reasoning is when you take thinking beyond what is needed or required.

required. The results of excessive reasoning is always confusion. Our own thinking processes can get tangled up with our intellect. This truth is revealed daily in the evolutionist's mind. They attempt to restructure the theory of evolution around facts that fail to hold water. Today, it is impossible to deny that a designer exits, yet classrooms of students are presented with confusing evidence of evolution. This excessive reasoning and lack of faith has painted the evolutionist into a corner. Their own reasoning will eventually destroy the theory of evolution.

Many scholars and intellectuals think that contentment and happiness come from knowing everything. That is contrary to what the Bible teaches. The Bible teaches that we should have faith when we cannot see the result of something. The very definition of faith is to trust or have confidence without evidence. We must believe before we know the outcome. That is what faith is. It is to understand the last portion of this verse:

Therefore be humbled under the mighty hand of God, so that He may exalt you in due time, casting all your anxiety onto Him, for He cares for you. (1 Peter 5:6–7, MKJV, emphasis added)

He cares for you! Faith requires that the outcome of our situations be in line with God's care for us. If God cares for us, the outcome of any situation will be okay.

For anxiety to take a back seat in your life, you need to have confidence in God without immediate evidence.

This may mean not knowing some things. This may mean not having a direct answer at hand. This may mean going about your busy day without a calculated plan, leaving things in the hands of God.

FREEDOM

A third noteworthy point in the Matthew 6 passage is that Jesus uses the illustration of birds of the air. Birds are the most unrestricted creatures on earth. The gift of flight is a bird's blessing. If you can imagine being able to fly, that in itself brings comfort from anxiety.

How is it possible for Jesus to compare us to birds? We all have restrictions, being bound by the things around us. Yet Jesus suggests that we can be as free as birds. Birds fly over obstructions and obstacles. They fly away from endangerment and threat. They have a great instinct about where to nest, where they are most protected from weather or predators.

Jesus tells us to look to the fowls of the air for our example. It becomes obvious that God has this place of freedom for us. Freedom is found in handling anxiety. Refuse those worrisome thoughts and you will experience freedom all around you.

GOD CARES

If anxiety has become a big problem in your life, Jesus wants you to know that God cares. The Message Bible puts it so clearly: *"Look at the birds, free and unfettered, not tied down to a job description, careless in the care of*

God. And you count far more to him than birds" (Matthew 6:26, MSG).

The words "careless in the care of God" mean that when we let go of the anxiety, He will step in and take over. When we decide to put our trust in His ability rather than our anxiety, He makes a way. God knows that we all struggle with anxiety, and He wants us to release it to Him.

The choice is ours. Can we let go of our cares, or do we keep them close to us in case something goes awry?

In addressing anxiety, Jesus reminded us that the only real way to be free from anxiety is to know God. Jesus had zero anxiety because He knew God.

In knowing God, we trust God totally and this trust overpowers anxiety. We know God well enough to trust Him no matter what the outcome of an event might be. That is the key—being unsure of the outcome, I can still live free. That's what I mean by keeping our feet on the neck of anxiety.

No one has an anxiety-free life. Anxiety will always pop up around us. Every one of us has things to be anxious about. You may have more than others, but if you know Jesus, you can know that God will make a way for you to be okay. The best place to keep it is underfoot, the farthest place from our thinking and from our hearts.

Guilt is your mind telling you that your conduct is unforgivable.

CHAPTER FOUR
Guilt

Brethren, I do not count myself to have apprehended; but one thing I do, forgetting those things which are behind and reaching forward to those things which are ahead, I press toward the goal for the prize of the upward call of God in Christ Jesus.

(Philippians 3:13–14)

GUILT HAS MAINLY TO DO WITH CONDEMNATION. Condemnation means to be declared guilty or to be doomed. It can also be described as blame. We blame ourselves, or maybe someone else blames us, for having made a mistake. We then declare ourselves guilty. It's impossible to change what happened, so it becomes impossible to be forgiven. The bottom line is this: can I really be forgiven for all that I've done, or not done?

Traditionally, guilt has been associated with our past, but guilt can also be related to the present and the future.

PEOPLE CAN FEEL GUILTY ABOUT THE FUTURE

People may feel guilty because they need to do something in the near future, either good or bad. Maybe they feel guilty because they know they cannot help another person in a time of crisis Perhaps they know they may have to say no to someone who's expecting them to come through for them down the road. Future guilt is also associated with a person believing they have not made good use of yesterday's time, which will affect their future.

PEOPLE CAN FEEL GUILTY ABOUT THE PRESENT

When I was growing up, it was articulated that enjoying something too much was a waste of time. Someone can feel guilty about doing something they enjoy, because they suppose they should be doing something more productive. They feel that they should be somewhere else, such as at work, in church, or with their family.

However, guilt about things that will happen in the future or are happening in the present can still be changed. They can be corrected and seen in the proper light. Change will begin to eradicate feelings of guilt.

The most difficult guilt to live with is past guilt, because our actions cannot be reversed. In this chapter, we will center on guilt that is brought on from past events.

PEOPLE OFTEN FEEL GUILTY ABOUT THE PAST

These can be trifling matters to others but life-sized to us. It includes everything from words spoken in anger to acting without thinking about the future, or even more consequential things such as assault, having an abortion, or having an extramarital affair. These can cause unrelenting guilt. People with past guilt are usually full of regret. They wish these things had never happened, but because they did happen they know they can never be changed.

CONSCIENCE AND FEELINGS

People fail to understand that the conscience part of our being was placed inside of us by God at creation. Its purpose is to be a guide or influence. When your conscience is bothering you, it's speaking to you about your actions or your possible actions. Your actions could be hurting or taking advantage of someone, including yourself.

When we fail to listen to our conscience, we end up doing something that can cause us guilt. Of course, we all know that the conscience can be overruled by justifying our actions with reason. We regularly see this in our judicial system, with participants on all sides using reason as the only defense. However, conscience was created so that we would know right from wrong, and no matter how much reason is assigned, some things are still wrong. Reason does not make everything right.

The conscience can only be attributed to a designer of right and wrong. Without a conscience, hurting others would be okay. We would fail to feel remorse for wrongdoing, and therefore have no guilt. God created the conscience to help us make decisions. However, He created feelings to help us understand our situation. No one should use feelings to make decisions.

CONSCIENCE AND HEART

There's a cool Bible verse that says, *"You created every part of me; you put me together in my mother's womb. I praise you because you are to be feared; all you do is strange and wonderful. I know it with all my heart"* (Psalms 139:13–14, GNT).

Paul reminded us that he lived in relation to his heart, or conscience. If anyone needed to get over guilt, it was Paul. He had rounded up Christians and had them tortured for their faith. Some were even killed for believing. Yet here he was, years later, walking in freedom from guilt: *"I thank God, whom I serve with a pure conscience, as my forefathers did…"* (2 Timothy 1:3)

If we are to be victorious in life, we need to allow our conscience to be our guide. I always suggest that people keep a tender conscience. Don't sear your conscience over time by committing the same sins over and over again. Timothy was told, *"Such teachings are spread by deceitful liars, whose consciences are dead, as if burnt with a hot iron"* (1 Timothy 4:2, GNT).

> I always suggest that people keep a tender conscience. Don't sear your conscience over time by committing the same sins over and over again.

By being continually resistant to the conscience's leading, it becomes possible to destroy the conscience. If we're honest with ourselves, we would say that our worst mistakes happened when we went against our conscience. The guilt of the past is created by not listening to our conscience. It is the guilt of the past that needs to be addressed.

THINGS HAPPEN

We begin to have feelings of guilt when we believe we've committed either a moral failure or a perceived social failure.

A moral failure has to do with offense, either against another person or our own moral fabric. The Bible identifies actions that are unacceptable, such as lying or unforgiveness. When we go against our moral principles, it produces feelings of guilt.

Social guilt has to do with not measuring up to someone else's expectations of us. We feel guilty because we don't have the things people seem to think we should have—a type of house, certain athletic abilities, or even our looks don't measure up. This creates thoughts of personal responsibility. Even though we might think other people are wrong about us, and we might even verbally resist them, inside we still feel responsible. This personal accountability then produces feelings of guilt.

Guilt can be triggered by the smallest of things. An event, a smell, or a song can bring back a bad memory. Or maybe it's a person's name being spoken. These can be clues that guilt has a place in our hearts, clues that we don't believe God has forgiven us.

We must all understand and know that no one has ever been guilt-free except for Jesus. Everyone has committed offense and has feelings of guilt. God knows that *"all have sinned and fall short of the glory of God"* (Romans 3:23).

GUILT ESCALATES

Guilt has the power to grow in us and cause unhappiness and sorrow. People with guilt issues envision the consequences of being exposed. They think, *If others find out what I did, they'll be disappointed in me. They could leave me or judge me for my actions.* The images they form in their mind becomes evil, unforgivable, and inexcusable. These images of unrealistic consequences filter into their thinking.

Sometimes guilty people even begin to imagine more than actually happened. They add to the memory. They can become consumed with regret and grief. It's not uncommon to find people who are crippled with anxiety and depression because of the guilt they feel. They think that they deserve to be punished.

GUILT BECOMES PUNISHMENT

Because it is impossible to change what happened, their punishment is a constantly nagging feeling of guilt, and people with a guilty conscious remind themselves of the mistake over and over to feel even more guilty. The guilt will pop up whenever they start to feel comfortable or begin to forget. In some way, they feel that the guilt compensates for the initial mistake.

The problem with this is that their self-worth is destroyed. Their self-esteem is challenged, affecting their self-image. It smothers their personality, originality, and individuality. People end up in a catch-22 where they have exciting things inside that they desire to accomplish, but they end up pushing those things back because of guilt. They measure themselves against the bar of the past. They think, *I failed in the past, so what has changed? I wasn't good enough to act properly in the past, so why do I deserve something good that could possibly change my life?*

The consequences of guilt are significant. People living with guilt usually fail to see that guilt is the root of the problem.

IS IT GOD?

Many people end up attributing these feelings to God. They think God controls the feelings inside them. Some even think that God speaks through feelings. This is far from reality, and far from God's intentions.

I wrote in the introduction that God doesn't withhold anything we may need. Jesus said, *"The thief does not come except to steal, and to kill, and to destroy. I have come that they may have life, and that they may have it more abundantly"* (John 10:10). Here we are taught that anything that steals, kills, or destroys is not from

God. Destructive feelings do not come from God. The thief refers to satan, God's archenemy, and he is the one attempting to stop us from accomplishing anything good, because we are God's greatest workmanship.

For we are His workmanship, created in Christ Jesus for good works, which God prepared beforehand that we should walk in them. (Ephesians 2:10)

Satan is attempting to deceive our thinking. He wants us to believe that our feelings of guilt are the truth. If he can get you to believe that guilt comes from God, he has won a small victory. A life full of regret and remorse is a small win for him, because he knows these feelings will stifle your success.

Guilt is the optimum emotion that satan uses to steal, kill, and destroy. The Bible calls this condemnation. All condemnation comes from satan. However, Paul reminds us, *"There is therefore now no condemnation to those who are in Christ Jesus, who do not walk according to the flesh, but according to the Spirit"* (Romans 8:1).

DON'T REVIVE WHAT IS INACTIVE

If we understand God at all, we will clearly see in the Bible that God doesn't use guilt to teach us anything. David clearly explains, *"As far as the east is from the west, so far has He removed our transgressions from us"* (Psalms 103:12). Isaiah tells us, *"For You have cast all my sins behind Your back"* (Isaiah 38:17), and Micah explains, *"You will be merciful to us once again. You will trample our sins underfoot and send them to the bottom of the sea!"* (Micah 7:19)

God is not a psychopath who one day removes and discards our sins and then has a change of heart, recovering them and sending them back to us in the form of guilt.

These accounts tell us that God doesn't remember our offences anymore. God makes a choice to forget our confessed sins. The only way to give our sins life is to reach behind God's back and recover them. In fact, they are irrecoverable to God. As John explains, *"[T]he blood of Jesus Christ His Son cleanses us from all sin"* (1 John 1:7). There is nothing more real to God than Jesus's sacrifice for our sins. When we ask forgiveness, His shed blood has enough power to remove and destroy all our sins from us eternally.

FORGIVE YOURSELF

As Christians, God forgives us for past transgressions when we ask Him. Isaiah says it so powerfully: *"The Lord says, 'Now, let's settle the matter. You are stained red with sin, but I will wash you as clean as snow. Although your stains are deep red, you will be as white as wool'"* (Isaiah 1:18). Never forget that there is forgiveness, healing, and restoration. God plays a part in the process, and so do we. God forgives us and we forgive ourselves. God begins the healing process and we accept the truth. Finally, God restores us to our original place and we accept His place for us.

Psychology has some good things to say about forgiving ourselves. Psychology asks, are we able to learn from the experiences we feel guilt over? Can we begin to see the bigger picture of how this affects those around us? Does our inability to forgive ourselves cause family members to struggle, including our children? Many times a person distressed with guilt can only see themselves and fails to see the consequences around them. They end up being more of a burden to others than they themselves believe they are.

The answer to these questions becomes this: can we forgive ourselves?

LETTING GO

The foundational scripture I used at the beginning of this chapter is key. It deals with fulfilling one's life purpose despite any mistakes we may have made. In Philippians 3:13–14, Paul plans to accomplish and finish a life full of satisfaction, contentment, and joy. He said, *"[T]he one thing I do, however, is to forget what is behind me and do my best to reach what is ahead"* (Philippians 3:13, GNT). In others words, it's our memory that creates feelings. We replay memories of our sins.

The guilt Paul could have carried would be all-consuming condemnation. Luke tells us that Paul himself said, *"I made trouble for everyone who followed the Lord's Way, and I even had some of them killed. I had others arrested*

and put in jail. I didn't care if they were men or women"
(Acts 22:4, CEV). Paul later became a Christian and had to
learn how to live with the guilt of his actions. His actions
had led to men and women being killed for the very truths
he came to accept on the Damascus road. This could have
created a guilt that choked the very life out of everything
he did. However, when we study his life we see some fun-
damental truths that caused Paul to become victorious.

RETURNING TO WHOLENESS

If you can move into these truths, you will begin to
heal just as God intends. Paul understood God by four
expressions: forgiveness, reconciliation, justification,
and righteousness. We can sum
up these words with one central
understanding: absolute love.
Absolute love is crucial to the
healing and restoration process.

> **Absolute love is crucial to the healing and restoration process.**

We must first know it, then understand it, and finally
accept it.

Natural love is never unconditional. It can sometimes
see beyond a transgression someone has made, but
only as long as it doesn't happen again. Absolute love
sees beyond these transgressions (broken boundaries)
and forgives, even if it happens again and again. If
someone loves you absolutely, it means that they are
never influenced or deterred by anything you have
done. In other words, your actions do not affect this
love. That's how God loves us.

ABSOLUTE LOVE

I thought I understood God's absolute (or unconditional) love.

One day, a question rose up inside me. I was working on a university Bible course called Counselling with Scripture. In the teaching lectures, the professor said that having a complete understanding of God's unconditional love is mandatory for the healing process to work. For someone to overcome issues of self-esteem or guilt, or even addictions, they need a full and complete grasp of God's love.

This is the question that posed itself to me in the middle of class, out of the blue: how do I know God loves me?

Later in my office, I reiterated the question to myself. In answering it, I used all the pat answers: "I received Jesus as my Lord and Savior. I'm trying my best to change for the better. The Bible tells me so." However, each time I answered I understood by scripture that the answer was wrong.

Suddenly, an analogy came to mind that I knew was from the Spirit of God.

If parents have twins and one twin reaches the heights of success in education, status, and profession while the other twin only achieves average accomplishments, which twin would they love more? The answer was easy. They would love both equally. But why? Why is this true for most normal, everyday parents? Even parents who are concerned about their children still love them unconditionally.

Why?

The answer I received from God was "Because they were born to them."

There was no other reason than that the children were born to the parents. Parental love is never contingent on what the children do or accomplish. It's never influenced by the mistakes the children make. It's not based on whether one is more reliable than the other. One is not perceived as good and the other bad.

The parents' love is based on the fact that their children were born, period. Having offspring produces a bond so powerful that it takes tremendous effort to break.

David said,

When I consider Your heavens, the work of Your fingers, the moon and the stars, which You have ordained, what is man that You are mindful of him, and the son of man that You visit him? For You have made him a little lower than the angels, and You have crowned him with glory and honor.

You have made him to have dominion over the works of Your hands; You have put all things under his feet, all sheep and oxen—even the beasts of the field, the birds of the air, and the fish of the sea that pass through the paths of the seas.

O Lord, our Lord, how excellent is Your name in all the earth! (Psalm 8:3–9)

Each and every person is born of God, and He loves them, no string attached. God loves His greatest creation and it has absolutely nothing to do with us accomplishing great things or being good. If you never go to church, never help a needy person, or never put a dollar in the offering plate, it will bear no weight on how much God loves you. His love only has to do with the fact that you were born.

Everyone who has ever been born was originally designed by God. Before your parents ever knew each other, God knew you. God told Jeremiah, *"I chose you before I gave you life..."* (Jeremiah 1:5, GNT, emphasis added) Jeremiah's life had a purpose, and each of us has a purpose; the purpose is to be part of God's family.

If you are alive on this earth, God loves you because He chose you to be born. You might think, *Well, He chose poorly. I've made too many mistakes. I've done too many bad things. I've messed up to many times to be forgiven.* That's the result of guilt, of not being able to see the whole truth of absolute love. As I said earlier, first you need to know it, then understand it, and finally accept it.

Suddenly, John 3:16 became so clear. God doesn't just love the good people or the kind people. God doesn't just love the Catholics or the Protestants. God doesn't just love the Jews, the Arabs, or the Americans. He loves the whole world, from the best of the best to the nastiest of the nastiest. Everyone who was ever born, everyone who is alive today, God loves.

It is our willingness to go our own way that breaks this relationship. However, the relationship is only broken on our end. It's never broken in God's eyes, heart, or mind. God never changes His unconditional love for any of us. He patiently waits until we are able to see how much He cares. He never intervenes or forces Himself into our lives. He waits.

The Bible says, *"We know what love is because Jesus gave his life for us"* (1 John 3:16, CEV). The reason Jesus gave His life was so that we would have the opportunity to accept God's unconditional love. Therefore, our need to fully understand repentance and receive this unconditional love is vital to our healing process. It's always there for the receiving. Jesus took our guilt and shame so we could have access to the Father. The Bible says, *"Much more then, having now been justified by His blood, we shall be saved from wrath through Him"* (Romans 5:9).

Intimidation is your mind telling you that you are inferior.

CHAPTER FIVE
Intimidation

For we dare not class ourselves or compare ourselves with those who commend themselves. But they, measuring themselves by themselves, and comparing themselves among themselves, are not wise.

(2 Corinthians 10:12, NKJV)

NOWADAYS, PEOPLE MOSTLY THINK ABOUT INTIMIDATION in the context of those who intimidate others—people who use their positions, talents, or money to coerce and bully.

Webster's Dictionary defines intimidate as "to make afraid; to inspire with fear; to dishearten; or to abash."[5] Abash is just an old word meaning to embarrass or shame. No one wants to feel ashamed, so they develop feelings of being threatened. In fact, the word intimidation comes from the word timid.

---

[5] Ibid, "Intimidate."

Individuals who feel intimided blame others rather than looking at themselves. *They think, If that person were not around to intimidate me, I wouldn't have these feelings.* This belief can be damaging to our future. In fact, intimidation usually exposes fears within ourselves. Intimidation exposes things like the fear of failure or the fear of rejection.

Usually the intimidated person learns to live with the feeling. They choose to believe that the weakness lies within the character of the intimidator, not themselves. When someone is overly concerned with what others think, this usually includes the feeling of intimidation.

NOT ALWAYS ABOUT PEOPLE

Intimidation isn't always about other people, though. It can be about our responsibilities. Sometimes we struggle with having to be accountable for our actions or having to live up to some expectation. Others may want to trust us with something, but the sheer scope of the responsibility intimidates us.

Intimidation can also be about position. Again, if a person continues to accept these feelings, they can begin to see themselves as weak. This type of intimidation commonly produces roots of failure. It's a mindset that says, "No matter what I put my hands to, it will probably fail. I have been unlucky in life and God didn't give me the talents or gifts or abilities He gave others."

STUFF

Intimidation can also be about thingamajigs. It affects lives by causing people to be timid, shy, and apprehensive. Timidity always creates trepidation, which includes the fear of embarking upon new activities, the fear of the unfamiliar, and the fear of making decisions.

The bottom line is that people neglect to try new things because of intimidation. I spent a season of my life as a farmer, growing various crops and livestock. Much of the new equipment that has been invented can be intimidating to learn. But a farmer needs to be careful not to allow new technology to intimidate him. Many older farmers have failed to pay the price for an expensive piece of equipment because it intimidates them. This in turn limited their production, beginning a slow decline in their business.

Feeling intimidated by things can bring about a slow deceleration in our lives. We think, *I may be the only one who's not able to operate or perform this correctly.* Our minds tell us that we can't do it.

My grandfather was one of the last people to use a threshing machine. Even I remember the threshing machine, because my grandfather used one into the 1960s, which is basically unheard of in Canada. He insisted on making sheaves because he didn't believe that a crop could dry properly on the ground. Every farmer for miles around began swathing crops to the ground rather than making sheaves. Eventually he was forced into purchasing a swather and combine because no one wanted to work a threshing machine. After a year or two, he realized the efficiency and became convinced. However, this delay affected the growth of his farm.

People, things, and responsibilities can seem too big, too perfect, or too unapproachable.

ABSOLUTELY

Intimidation can be felt absolutely or silently. By absolutely, I mean that we know when we feel it. It's right in the forefront of our emotions, challenging us and telling us, "This is way too big." We begin to think we cannot do something or even make a decision. We don't think we can live up to other people's expectations. We think, *I'm not as good at this as someone else is.*

The intimidation forces us to pull back. We know when we feel this way, and we want to run and hide from it.

This comes from thinking someone else is better than we are, from believing we are inferior or unacceptable.

Absolute intimidation can come from a person in authority. It can also come from someone more popular or seemingly more outgoing. Maybe it's someone who seems better at doing what we're learning.

SILENTLY

With silent intimidation, we are intimidated by certain things, responsibilities, or people and are unsure why. In our thoughts, we sabotage advancement rather than facilitate it. We're unsure why, because nothing has been done to us. It's just that we feel we could be embarrassed or shamed in this area given a chance.

Intimidation is a form of insecurity, an attack on our confidence. We doubt who we are, think we're not smart enough, not good enough, not talented or polished enough to keep up. We fail to see that we're gifted and valuable.

Even in the face of possible hurt, Peter had to tell the people in the church in Asia Minor not to allow intimidation to affect their lives:

But even if you should suffer for the sake of righteousness, you are blessed. And do not fear their intimidation, and do not be troubled... (1 Peter 3:14, NASB)

Someone else may be more aggressive or have a more outgoing personality, but that shouldn't affect us. They may seem to have more money or position or education, but that shouldn't cause us to look down on ourselves.

How can we begin to change this destructive attitude?

ACKNOWLEDGE INTIMIDATION

Once a person can acknowledge that they have intimidation issues, change becomes possible. An addicted person cannot begin to recover until they recognize that they have a problem.

The reason intimidation can be so powerful is that many people refuse to admit they have a problem in the first place. It can become second nature to always blame someone or something else for the way they feel. Can someone stubbornly look at themselves and see the mechanisms of intimidation?

Feeling intimidated doesn't necessarily mean being quiet and shy. People under the influence of intimidation can learn to deflect the intimidation by using defense mechanisms. This can be exposed in defensive remarks, dishonor, and sharp words. They fight to keep intimidation at bay and unknowingly obstruct themselves from fulfilling their dreams or goals in life.

If intimidation can be seen as playing a bigger role in life than most people give it credit for, change can happen. People can look at an event and say, "That intimidated me. I challenge myself next time to not be intimidated. Even if I'm not as good as the next person, I will step out and try."

CONTENTMENT

Intimidation plays a major role in our contentment, and I believe that a majority of people are looking for contentment. Everyone wants to be at peace, happy in life.

To be in contentment is to be resting, satisfied, and thankful. When a person finds contentment, intimidation takes a back seat. There's no competition anymore. A content person looks for ways to move forward personally and change things, and they're always thankful. They feel good with who they are and where they're at.

The Bible prompts us to find contentment. Each person needs to find it for themselves.

Paul said, *"Not that I speak in regard to need, for I have learned in whatever state I am, to be content..."* (Philippians 4:11) And the writer of Hebrews reminded us that Jesus said, *"Let your conduct be without covetousness; be content with such things as you have. For He Himself has said, 'I will never leave you nor forsake you'"* (Hebrews 13:5).

Jesus will never abandon or disown you because you didn't live up to or accomplish a certain standard. He came and died for our sins so that we could have a life of contentment and purpose. This purpose is never to someone else's standard. Rather, it's a standard that set in the Word of God.

STOP COMPARISON

Intimidation comes from comparing one's life to another. Many people compare how they look, what they know, what they own, and what they do. Comparing yourself to others will lead to a belief that the other person has accomplished more; therefore that person is better at life.

John shared about Jesus and Peter, an experience he had. It happened after Jesus had been raised from the dead and had returned to earth to teach His disciples. The complete text is found in John 21:15–25. Jesus was explaining to Peter about his future:

"Most assuredly, I say to you, when you were younger, you girded yourself and walked where you wished; but when you are old, you will stretch out your hands, and another will gird you and carry you where you do not wish." This He spoke, signifying by what death he would glorify God. And when He had spoken this, He said to him, "Follow Me." (John 21:18–19)

Peter thought, *Well, if this is going to happen to me, what's going to happen to my friend John?* So he asked Jesus to compare what he had to do with what John had to do.

Peter, seeing him, said to Jesus, "But Lord, what about this man?" (John 21:21)

Interestingly Jesus said to Peter, "You just go ahead and accomplish your life. Leave John to accomplish what he needs to accomplish and you accomplish what you need to accomplish." Jesus was telling Peter to stay on track with his life, and not to worry about John: "I have a plan for you and I have a plan for John. It's not the same as yours. Everyone has something different to accomplish. You guys are different, with different purposes, different gifts, and different reasons for being born."

Many times, our intimidation comes from a belief that someone else does what we do better than us.

However, we all have different graces and abilities. Most times when we compare ourselves to someone else we're stepping outside of God's purpose for us. It's not uncommon for people to try to copy others, but this produces an inferior copy. You are an original.

SEE DIVERSITY

It's like a professional chess player saying he's no good in life because he can't play professional hockey. The chess player's talent lies in solving problems and seeing much farther down the game. The hockey player is more skilled in the moment, taking advantage of fitness and athletic skill. It's a different game with a different set of talents and skills. Each person needs to find their place and accept their place. Too many people who suffer from intimidation are trying to be someone they're not. Paul said,

> *For I say, through the grace given to me, to everyone who is among you, not to think of himself more highly than he ought to think, but to think soberly, as God has dealt to each one a measure of faith. For as we have many members in one body, but all the members do not have the same function...* (Romans 12:3)

When we step outside our character, we can begin to feel intimidation.

PURPOSE

We were created to fulfill an original design from God, and when we don't fulfill it we feel like something is lacking. Intimidation steals from us by not allowing us to use our God-given abilities, gifts, and talents.

Many people don't realize the power of intimidation, yet it has influenced their lives.

I knew one man who wanted to be an usher at church but was intimidated by what he thought people would think of him. He thought people would stare because he was too big. The crowd was intimidating to him. However, after he got over the intimidation and started to be an usher he met a woman from church who became his wife. Up to that point, the intimidation had affected his very confidence to even try to find a wife.

Someone may have the gift of hospitality and be fearful that they cannot live up to another person's level of hospitality, so they refuse to invite anyone over. A person may love to give but fear that their gift won't measure up to what others have given.

Just accept that God has made each person unique and distinct. Every one of us has available to us all the things we need to fulfill a life of purpose. God didn't forget or leave anything out.

Of course, we all need to work on and polish those bestowed gifts and abilities, but always start where you're at. Don't forget to look at what you have. You are genuine, an original, and a favorite of God. How do I know? Because you are here on earth. God desired for you to be born and there is a divine plan for you which is intended to last throughout eternity.

IT'S NOT ABOUT ACCOMPLISHMENTS

People often measure themselves only by their accomplishments, but this is very deceiving. Intimidation stems from not knowing who you are in Christ. Maybe someone tried something and didn't get to first base, so they assumed it was their fault. They think they're not smart enough or talented enough to achieve their goal.

> People often measure themselves only by their accomplishments, but this is very deceiving. Intimidation stems from not knowing who you are in Christ.

The devil and Jesus once had a conversation:

> And the devil said to Him, "If You are the Son of God, command this stone to become bread."
> But Jesus answered him, saying, "It is written, 'Man shall not live by bread alone, but by every word of God.'" (Luke 4:3–4)

Notice how satan attempted to intimidate Him, questioning Jesus to see if He really believed and understood His place. How did satan intimidate? By telling Jesus to prove Himself. It was a smokescreen to intimidate Jesus into doing something outside of God's plan.

Intimidation can affect many areas of your life, but the most serious is your freedom to be who God created you to be. People always feel as though they need to prove themselves. They feel like no one will see them unless they can perform to an acceptable degree.

The devil knows what intimidates us and attempts to use it against us. Be careful not to be tricked into thinking you must always do something to prove yourself. Don't think, *I must do something to get God to be happy with me. I must do something to show others I'm not a failure.* Jesus knew who He was. Of course He could turn stones into bread, but He wasn't going to be intimidated into obeying the devil.

We must all know who we are. We're so much more than our perceived accomplishments and external appearances. That's one of the main reasons the Bible is so important. It explains how God sees people and how we grow in our individuality.

You need to ask yourself, *Am I able to see myself the way God sees me?* The only possible way to enjoy life and relish each day is to look at yourself in the light of God's creation. Once we become satisfied with who we are, it's amazing how quickly intimidation will take a back seat. We'll be able to step out and begin to change and grow where once we would have been afraid.

NUMBER ONE PRIORITY

God created us for relationship with Him, and the master plan is a life together with Him. His blessing is connected to this relationship. His blessing is attached to us by our believing that He knows all things, that He created all things and understands how all things work. It is very important to know that God is always for us, as Romans 8 so marvelously proclaims:

And we know that God causes all things to work together for good to those who love God, to those who are called according to His purpose... What then shall we say to these things? If God is for us, who is against us? (Romans 8:28, 31, NASB)

We can place so much value on this earthly life that we forget about our most important relationship: the Father God relationship. He has a plan and we want to do our best to be all we can be in this life.

But this life is a short beginning to a life of eternity. Many people have done notable things, but here on earth we don't even know who they are. Margret E. Knight invented the foldable paper bag. Other than family, no one remembers. Eugene Polley invented the remote control we use every day. These are all great natural conveniences, but they have no eternal value. The only eternal value these people may have is that they may have received Jesus as Lord. They may have used their resources to further God's plan for their lives and others.

God wants us to accomplish good things on this earth, even become successful and prosperous, but the goal is bigger than you. The goal is for you to use what you are blessed with to further the lives of others, whether that's through your finances, talents, skills, or position.

God has an eternal plan for each person and that's why the devil loves to intimidate. Intimidation can hinder us from getting to the place our Father desires for us. The great thing about God is that He can work with each of us individually.

TEAMWORK

A very important consideration in overcoming the fear of intimidation is teamwork. The God-team of Father, Son, Holy Spirit, and us works to accomplish the

> The God-team of Father, Son, Holy Spirit, and us works to accomplish the calling from deep within our spirit.

calling from deep within our spirit. If you've accepted Jesus as your Savior and Lord, you are part of this team.

The Bible explains that God consists of the Father, Son, and Holy Spirit, and that we are in Him and He is in us. Together, we are an inseparable team.

Jesus said, *"I will ask the Father, and he will give you another Helper, who will stay with you forever"* (John 14:16, GNT). That helper is the Holy Spirit and He lives within us when we decide to accept Jesus as Savior and Lord.

We need to trust this God team: God the creator of the universe, Jesus who paid the debt of our sin, and the Holy Spirit who guides our life. When we take the time to consider this team, we'll realize that we are complete. Nothing else is required. All other things will fall into place when this team functions at full capacity.

Our family, our career, our future, and our eternity are all dependent on the priority we place on God.

This is the only way to find satisfaction. Satisfaction will trample intimidation under its feet. God knows that our emotional health is dependent on our purpose and satisfaction. He made it that way, for us to stay dependent on Him.

God wants to work with people and through people. Don't allow anyone to tell you that Jesus is just a crutch. Of course we depend on Him, but that dependency creates a relationship, which creates satisfaction. The world is looking for satisfaction and cannot find it because it's impossible to find apart from God.

Trust that God has your best interests at heart. Remember: *"What then shall we say to these things? If God is for us, who is against us?"* (Romans 8:31, NASB) In order to fulfill such a plan for our lives, intimidation needs to take a back seat.

WHAT DOES IT MEAN TO TRUST

Overcoming intimidation takes trust in the team. If there's one thing a team has to have, it's trust. Once there is mistrust, a team begins to break down. Every member of the team must trust the others—from a sports team to a family team or the God-team. Trust is vital to the outcome. No matter what kind of team you're part of, trust holds it all together.

Trust means "confidence: a reliance or resting of the mind on the integrity, veracity, justice, friendship, or other sound principles of another person."[6] Real trust depends on God. Many people say they trust God, but if you look at their lives it's just not there. They only go to God for the impossible, but if anything is naturally possible they will try those methods first.

There's so much knowledge today that there are many things a person can try first, before God. People trust the law for security, and economics for financial protection. We can go to counselors for emotional health and medical science for physical health. We get an education to get a job, and we turn to family and friends for favors. On and on it goes.

Not too many Christians just go ahead and trust God for everything in life, yet we see many examples in the Bible of men and women of old just trusting God for down-to-earth things. Simple things like help with intimidation.

I'm reminded of David, who trusted God and asked for the sort of simple and ordinary things we sometimes think are unimportant. David proclaimed and prayed for everyday concerns in his life. He, too, was affected by intimidation. He asked God to help him not to feel embarrassed. He asked God not to feel ashamed or confused.

Many people fail to realize that they can trust the God-team for these things, yet they are available within us. Having protection means so much more than bodily safety. It's about more than protection for family, for finances, and for our futures. Protection also means security of our mind, character, and actions.

---

[6] Ibid., "Trust."

O my God, I trust in You; let me not be ashamed.
(Psalms 25:2)

In thee, O Lord, do I put my trust: let me never be put to confusion. (Psalms 71:1, KJV)

I trust in God and am not afraid; I praise him for what he has promised. What can a mere human being do to me? (Psalms 56:4, GNT)

When we step out and attempt something new, God wants to help. When we need safety, God wants to help. When we set our aim to accomplish something, God wants to help. When we are intimidated to start or try something, God wants to help.

I've used these scriptures many times, especially when I need to make important decisions or when I'm going to be speaking publically. I know that I don't want to be ashamed. I want and need to be able to trust God in all areas of my life.

In order for us to be trustworthy team players, we must trust God to come through for us. I've noticed that when I trust Him, everything turns out fine, even if I make a mistake or mess up. The God-team works together because they care.

Trust brings a peace and ease to life. I like to call it being content.

Lies are your mind defending your struggles and challenges.

CHAPTER SIX

Lies

*Just say "Yes" or "No"—anything else you say
comes from the Evil One.*
(Matthew 5:37, GNT)

IS IT POSSIBLE IN THIS INSINCERE AND SELF-CENTERED CULTURE
to be a person of probity, integrity, and good faith? In
this chapter, we want to look at two very specific areas.
The first is *the father of all lies*, whom we all know as
satan. Most people fail to understand that every untruth
originates with the devil. However, the responsibility of
believing or rejecting these lies falls to us.

The second part of this chapter will deal with
individual honesty. This area is called *truthfulness*.

THE LIES OF THE SATAN

The only way a person will believe in a lie is by not
knowing the truth. For instance, if you know what
the color red looks like, it would be impossible for
you to believe the lie that the words written on this

page are written in red ink. If not, you could believe it. Therefore, the only way to believe a lie is to be tricked or deceived.

We find this type of deception throughout society. Many businesses, media outlets, and even people with whom we have relationships use our ignorance to trick us. This is also satan's main tactic.

SPIRITUAL REALITY

Many people are unaware that the realm of the spirit is the original realm. They think that the natural realm is the original realm, yet the Bible is clear that the opposite is true. In fact, if we would just take a bit of time to comprehend this truth, we would realize that spiritual things created natural things. God created from His spirit realm everything we now live in on this earth.

Genesis records that the last thing God created was mankind, which is dirt on the outside and spirit on the inside.

> *Then God said, "Let Us make man in Our image, according to Our likeness; let them have dominion over the fish of the sea, over the birds of the air, and over the cattle, over all the earth and over every creeping thing that creeps on the earth." So God created man in His own image; in the image of God He created him; male and female He created them.* (Genesis 1:26–27)

Then the Lord God took some soil from the ground and formed a man out of it; he breathed life-giving breath into his nostrils and the man began to live. (Genesis 2:7, GNT)

How did he do that? You'll have to be like me and believe this by faith and personal knowledge of God. Everyone will get a chance to ask Him, if they would like, because there's a one hundred percent chance of death. Everyone dies. The author of the book of Hebrews writes, *"And as it is appointed for men to die once, but after this the judgment..."* (Hebrews 9:27) We all know that the human body, with all its tissues and organs, stays here on earth after we die, yet the spirit lives on.

The point I'm attempting to get across is that the spiritual realm is very, very real. To grasp the truth that satan has influence in our lives is to know that the spiritual realm has the ability to influence the natural realm.

THE FATHER OF LIES

Jesus confirmed this when He said that the devil is the father of lies. Jesus was speaking to people who were believing and agreeing with satan's lies. They were religious people, arguing that Jesus was from the devil rather than from God. Jesus responded that they were believing a lie:

You are of your father the devil, and the desires of your father you want to do. He was a murderer from the beginning, and does not stand in the truth, because there is no truth in him. When he speaks a lie, he speaks from his own resources, for he is a liar and the father of it. (John 8:44)

Jesus very clearly confirms that when satan speaks, he is lying. It's not a matter of *if* he might speak; Jesus acknowledged the fact that satan speaks to people. The

> **Jesus very clearly confirms that when satan speaks, he is lying.**

question should not be about satan's ability to speak. The question is, how will we respond when he does?

ONE SOURCE FOR ALL LIES

All lies begin at one source: satan. We can see the beginning of lies in the Garden of Eden, where sin originated—and it originated from a lie. Notice what Genesis says about the devil: *"The snake replied, 'That's not true; you will not die. God said that because he knows that when you eat it, you will be like God and know what is good and what is bad"* (Genesis 3:4–5, GNT).

This was a lie. Adam and Eve were deceived by a lie, from satan, which led to instant spiritual death. This was a deception, because part of satan's words were true—they *would* know good and evil—but the other part of his words were lies. God clearly warned Adam and Eve against eating from the tree, because it would cause death, yet satan said it would not.

*And the Lord God commanded the man, saying,
"Of every tree of the garden you may freely eat;
but of the tree of the knowledge of good and evil
you shall not eat, for in the day that you eat of it
you shall surely die." (Genesis 2:16–17)*

God knew that having an understanding of good and evil would be more harmful to them than not knowing. Even so, the choice remained Adam's and Eve's, and they believed satan's lie over God's Word.

LYING THOUGHTS

In the New Testament, Jesus revealed how satan operates, and how he lies. Looking at the story of Judas, we read, *"Jesus and his disciples were at supper. The Devil had already put into the heart of Judas, the son of Simon Iscariot, the thought of betraying Jesus"* (John 13:2, GNT). Notice that satan implanted in Judas just the *thought* of betraying Jesus. First comes the thought, then the action.

It seems that people can believe that God speaks. What's troubling is that people don't recognize that satan also speaks—through thoughts. Just as God speaks to our spirit from the spiritual realm, the devil speaks from the thought realm. With Judas, it was a thought.

FIRST THE THOUGHT

The thought must take place before a person allows it to enter into their heart. As the Bible describes, it is necessary to deal with these thoughts quickly, by rejecting lies before there's a chance they might get more deeply rooted in the heart, as with Judas.

The Bible is clear that knowing the Word of God is the safest, most powerful and intelligent position to hold.

The word of God is alive and active, sharper than any double-edged sword. It cuts all the way through, to where soul and spirit meet, to where joints and marrow come together. It judges the desires and thoughts of the heart. (Hebrews 4:12, GNT)

Notice that the Word of God cuts through the confusion of the soul realm (where our thinking takes place) and the spiritual realm (where the real you exists). Satan loves to trick us into entering the realm of thinking and feeling. We need to deal with satan's lies at the intellectual level.

See, the devil speaks, and when he does speak it's a lie. If we don't know the truth, we can be easily tricked into believing his lies. You cannot believe a lie if you know the truth. This has everything to do with knowing the truth of God's Word.

PERSONAL ATTACKS

Satan loves personal attacks. His goal is to get you to reject God by attacking you personally. He knows that if you believe his lies, you are on your way to rejecting the Word of God.

Knowing that satan speaks, we can see that all these fragilities we've looked at so far in this book stem from the lies of satan. Fear is a lie that tricks us into thinking our future is uncertain. Rejection is a lie that tricks us into thinking we are unloved. Anxiety is a lie that tricks us into thinking the outcome is unsure. Guilt is a lie that tricks us into thinking our conduct is unforgivable. Intimidation is a lie that tricks us into thinking we are inferior. By lying, we are tricked into thinking we are protecting ourselves. Excuses, which we'll cover in the next chapter, is a lie that tricks us into thinking we're not responsible.

These are all lies of the devil. When people believe them, they become fragile. All these lies are contrary to the Word of God. As The Message Bible says, *"When the Liar speaks, he makes it up out of his lying nature and fills the world with lies"* (John 8:44, MSG).

KNOW THE BIBLE

The warnings in the Bible are real:

> *Therefore submit to God. Resist the devil and he will flee from you.* (James 4:7)

> *...nor give place to the devil.* (Ephesians 4:27)

Also see 1 Peter 5:8–9, Ephesians 6:11, and 1 Timothy 3:7. The Bible warns us over and over again that it is possible for us to be deceived. It is our responsibility to not frivolously go through life without assessing our thoughts. Are they true or lies?

The ball is in our court. It is our responsibility to know the Bible and what the Bible says about us. I have provided examples and quotes from the Bible numerously in this book, but there is so much more to know. If I could summarize the Bible's truths about who you are, it would be based on this scripture:

What marvelous love the Father has extended to us! Just look at it—we're called children of God! That's who we really are. But that's also why the world doesn't recognize us or take us seriously, because it has no idea who he is or what he's up to. (1 John 3:1, MSG)

So many people fail to see and understand this essential fact. Satan is an active enemy. His hatred for God makes him loathe us, so God put some things into His Word to help us see truth—the truth that we are children of God. If you have received Jesus as Lord, you are a child of God, and as His child you have access to His promises.

A SUMMARY IN BRIEF OF HIS PROMISES

Here is a summary of the Bible's truths for us to know and receive. This will help not only with knowing the difference between truth and untruth, but also with knowing what your Father God says about you.

- I am a new creature in Christ Jesus and have been accepted by God.
- I am a child of God.
- I am Jesus's friend and have been set free.
- I am God's incredible work of art and am totally and completely forgiven.
- I am chosen, holy, and blameless before God.
- I have been given an inheritance and am already seen as seated with Christ Jesus in heavenly places.
- I am a citizen of heaven, greatly loved, and God will never condemn me.
- I produce good works on earth and God supplies all my needs.
- I can go to God in prayer and have peace that guards my heart and mind.
- I have been made complete in Christ and God loves me and has chosen me.

ANY MEANS POSSIBLE

The devil's method is to tell one lie at a time, one person at a time. He attempts to change the culture of the world this way. If satan cannot get you to believe a lie about yourself, he'll try to get someone else to convey the message. We've all been there, when others seem to help us see our faults and mistakes. They seemingly point out all our weaknesses.

Satan has no stage and no microphone to speak his lies from. He does, however, have this pathway into a person's mind. If he can get a person to believe a lie, he has their stage and their microphone to speak from. In order for him to get us to think lies about ourselves, he uses other people, events, and wrong judgments. I've seen people believe lies from the TV, the internet, celebrities, teachers, friends, and bullies. He tries to fill our world with doubt and gray areas—doubts about our abilities, our beliefs, our futures, our looks, our friends, our families, our whole being.

Don't fall for the trap. Don't have anything to do with lies, half-truths, and confusion. Know God and know how God sees you.

TRUTHFULNESS

This second part of this chapter is hard to write, because it deals with our individual honesty. Honesty is an abused word these days. Most people don't see themselves as phonies because they define honesty in their own eyes. They have a drive to be seen as competent, capable, and adept, and this causes them to define honesty differently.

Over the years, such people have convinced themselves that there are acceptable ways to lie. This includes everything from photoshopped pictures to exaggerating or understating details. People can think that telling little white lies is a necessary tool if they believe it is in service of a bigger purpose. The problem is that the bigger purpose is usually to protect oneself.

Everyone wants to look good. As I said in Chapter Two, we all want to avoid rejection. However, stepping into the arena of dishonesty isn't acceptable. Everyone needs to be honest with themselves, taking the time to reflect by looking at how and why they say or do things.

I have needed to be careful about wanting to exaggerate. The more I used certain personal stories as an application in teaching, the more I wanted to build up those stories to be more than they really were. The more dramatic and interesting the story, the better I could look. That left the impression with people that I had something to do with the good outcome, when in all reality I would have fallen flat if not for the grace of God.

It's surprising how lies weave a web of deception. People can become deceived by their own lies, robbing them of their inner peace and forcing them to live up to the exaggeration. They begin to believe the falsehood, which in turn affects their day-to-day lives.

PLAIN OLD DISHONESTY

> There is dishonest communication, dishonest actions, and dishonest thinking.

Lies come in so many different forms. There is dishonest communication, dishonest actions, and dishonest thinking.

With dishonest communication, we can encounter problems like a failure to disclose, to mislead by withholding information. Some people think that a failure to disclose is lying while others say that it's okay to leave out certain things. Some believe if they were to explain every detail of a story, it would only cause confusion.

Others say everything needs to be in the open in order for people to make good choices.

In other words, some people rationalize. They might say, "If someone had asked for the full truth, I would have given it. But they didn't, so the fault is theirs."

Do you believe it's lying if you sell someone a car with a bad transmission if the buyer fails to ask you about the transmission? Proverbs confronts dishonesty head-on:

The riches you get by dishonesty soon disappear, but not before they lead you into the jaws of death. (Proverbs 21:6)

People manipulate words in conversation or public speech to leave a certain impression. Many times the desired impression has a self-centered purpose. They hope to get way with things by not sharing all the facts. Similarly, they can manipulate their words to cover up something they did or did not do.

The failure to disclose seems like a good way to protect one's reliability, but in fact it eats away at one's honesty.

These days, it has become popular to misrepresent ourselves to impress others. Social media scam is all about falling into the appearance trap. Good people who have great lives try hard to impress their family, friends, and others. It's as though they are attempting to say, "Look at me. I fit in with the rest of you."

The need to look better is a sign of a bigger problem. It's a fragility, exposing their thinking for what it is. In an attempt to impress, they're really saying that they have concerns about their self-worth. Needing to look good exposes a hole in their lives, revealing insecurities, a lack of confidences, and discontentment.

In order to change your perspective, you must be willing to learn how to be a person of integrity.

INTEGRITY

Integrity should be our standard for life, not outward appearances. Our desire to follow God's will for our lives has to include integrity.

Integrity of the heart is the result of having a fulfilled and content life. We must have integrity with ourselves when no one is looking, and integrity when dealing with others and their properties.

Webster's explains that a person of integrity is a person of "wholeness and soundness,"[7] a person who deals honestly in all mutual dealings and in the affairs of others.

The author of Proverbs explains, *"Better is the poor who walks in his integrity than one who is perverse in his lips, and is a fool"* (Proverbs 19:1). A life of integrity brings a wholeness and soundness to every day. It brings the confidence and security everyone is looking for. It's easy to live with yourself when you walk with integrity.

---

[7] Ibid., "Integrity."

Biblically, integrity means that we do what we say. If we say something, we follow through with it. According to the Bible, words are the most powerful tool God has given us. How can we believe in the integrity of God if we ourselves do not have integrity?

WARNINGS

I'm always surprised when I read about the warnings in the Bible about lying. One of the Ten Commandments is *"You shall not bear false witness against your neighbor"* (Deuteronomy 5:20). In fact, the word to lie is the Greek word *pseudomai*, meaning "falsely, lie, lied, and lying."[8] Thayer's dictionary defines the word "to lie, to speak deliberate falsehoods, to deceive one by a lie or to lie to."[9]

Most of the New Testament is written to Christians. I often wonder how born-again, Bible-believing people could tell lies, yet it is addressed many times in the Bible. Paul had this to say to the church in Colosse: *"Do not lie to one another, since you have put off the old man with his deeds"* (Colossians 3:9). He also told the church in Ephesus: *"Therefore, putting away lying, 'Let each one of you speak truth with his neighbor,' for we are members of one another"* (Ephesians 4:25). Obviously, slipping into dishonesty is much easier than many people believe.

---

[8] *New American Standard Exhaustive Concordance*, Updated Edition, "Pseudomai" (La Habra, CA: The Lockman Foundation, 1988).

[9] J.H. Thayer, *Thayer's Greek Definitions* (1896). As found on www.e-sword.net.

Truth and integrity is a big deal to God. However, the biggest problem with dishonesty is dealing with ourselves after we've been dishonest. We will be stamped with disapproval and emotional instability, simply because we will know that we've done wrong. If not repented of, dishonesty will breed more dishonesty. Why? Because we'll feel the need to prove our untruth or exaggeration.

THE SLIPPERY SLOPE

Judas Iscariot is an extreme example of a dishonest person who eventually believed his own lies and destroyed himself. He became a betrayer of everything good.

There's a specific incident in the Bible which exposes his true heart: when he openly scolded Jesus about a decision He had made. Dishonesty is usually connected to selfishness or self-preservation, and Judas saw an opportunity, but it slipped away from him and his dishonest heart was revealed. Judas said,

"Why wasn't this perfume sold for three hundred silver coins and the money given to the poor?" He said this, not because he cared about the poor, but because he was a thief. He carried the money bag and would help himself from it. (John 12:5–6, GNT)

It is possible for dishonesty to grow, never seeing the consequences it produces.

Jesus was still speaking when a crowd arrived, led by Judas, one of the twelve disciples. He came up to Jesus to kiss him. But Jesus said, "Judas, is it with a kiss that you betray the Son of Man?" (Luke 22:47–48, GNT)

If we follow the story to completion, Judas betrayed Jesus for thirty pieces of silver. However, once he understood that he himself had believed the lie that Jesus was a fraud, it ended in his demise.

When Judas, the traitor, learned that Jesus had been condemned, he repented and took back the thirty silver coins to the chief priests and the elders. "I have sinned by betraying an innocent man to death!" he said.

"What do we care about that?" they answered. "That is your business!"

Judas threw the coins down in the Temple and left; then he went off and hanged himself. (Matthew 27:3–5, GNT)

As I said, this is an extreme example of dishonesty and its results. It's a fair warning about what can happen when you enter the slippery slope of dishonesty.

YEA/YEA AND NAY/NAY

Jesus said, *"Do not even swear by your head, because you cannot make a single hair white or black. Just say*

'Yes' or 'No'—anything else you say comes from the Evil One" (Matthew 5:36–37, GNT).

When we look at the exact meaning of this scripture, we see that our instruction is to be honest and straightforward in our speech. Can we speak without evasion or beating around the bush? Can we be candid, frank, and truthful?

If you don't know the answer to something, just be honest and say, "I don't know." People take liberties in answering questions, sometimes just guessing and leaving the impression that it is a real answer. It's a factor of pride. Jesus reminds us that if we cannot answer with certainty, because we are uncertain, it's okay to say so.

Everyone needs to be careful about pride, as pride sometimes causes us to leave a wrong impression. This falls into the category of an untruth.

An inability to be honest can also be a pride issue.

He who is of a proud heart stirs up strife, but he who trusts in the Lord will be prospered. (Proverbs 28:25)

Excuses are your mind telling you that you are not responsible.

CHAPTER SEVEN

Excuses

Don't procrastinate—
there's no time to lose.
(Proverbs 6:4, MSG)

TALKING ABOUT EXCUSES IS A FITTING WAY TO CONCLUDE
this book. When people fail to limit the adverse effects
of being fragile, they make excuses. Excuses are made
to cover up feelings of fear, rejection, anxiety, guilt, and
intimidation.

A careful look at these fragile traits begins to reveal
why we make excuses. Our desire for acceptance may
lead us to make excuses. When we feel intimated or
afraid, we can generate excuses to protect us from
feeling afraid or unwanted. This can be a defense against
the dread of pain and hurt.

Excuses evolve into more than spoken and verbal
explanations. Over time, they become second nature,
becoming habits that affect the rest of our lives.

PROCRASTINATION

For people who dread certain outcomes, dilatory tactics can become the norm. Procrastination, delays, and being tardy are all forms of excuses. When we put things off until a later date, we're sending a loud message: "I do not like this" or "I am uncomfortable in this area."

The problem with stalling is that it becomes a lifestyle. The person becomes so accustomed to putting things off that eventually their whole life is on hold, doing a little here and a little there just to get by. They fail to take responsibility for the future.

Jesus instructed us to take responsibility even for things that are small and may not even belong to us:

And if you have not been faithful with what belongs to someone else, who will give you what belongs to you? (Luke 16:12, GNT)

RESPONSIBILITY

Responsibility is a key to successful living. Taking responsibility means being able to see that excuses are linked to our perception of how we see ourselves.

No matter how many opportunities come our way, the only way to success is through taking responsibility. Solomon explains, *"Catch the foxes, the little foxes, before they ruin our vineyard in bloom"* (Song of Solomon 2:15, GNT). Excuses are like the little foxes that spoil the garden.

The analogy is that our life is a vineyard in bloom. When a vineyard is in bloom, it's the little things that can come in and mess up the blossoms. They don't seem like a big deal, but over time they ruin the garden's potential. The little foxes seem so innocent and enjoyable, yet when they come in and play among the vines they knock the blossoms off. Fewer blossoms produce fewer grapes.

God wants to take us from being in bloom to producing an orchard. However, excuses disrupt the growth, messing up our opportunities and destroying our potential.

SEEMS RIGHT

The word excuse means to release someone from an obligation, undertaking or duty. However, the excuse is usually intended to release us from responsibilities or obligations that need to get done, or to get us out of doing something we don't want to do. Excuses are also used to release us from the accountability of our bad decisions or mistakes. People make excuses in every area of life, including family, the workplace, and most importantly God.

When we make excuses, we think those excuses are a valid reason for not accepting the challenge. They feel like we're making a valid alternative. They seem right. They seem like they're no big deal!

A CLOSER LOOK

However, excuses become a big deal when they affect our potential. Many people use excuses because they feel inadequate, incapable of realizing a dream or ambition. Maybe there's something they would like to achieve, but they feel deficient or limited. Rather than face the challenge head on, they make excuses to skirt the challenge. It's easier to maintain the status quo than try to change or excel. It's easier to stay where they are rather than step out into the unknown.

But God never intended for us to be status quo people.

When I look at my life and the times I've made excuses, they were always used to justify a perceived failure. I can easily see how excuses justify our feelings of being unsuccessful.

This became clear after my decision to go to Bible school and become a minister. When things didn't go as expected, when they took longer than expected, or when no one seemed to understand what I thought was important, excuses were like a sedative. My aspirations to have a ministry were taking too long. What I thought would be a quick process slowly became ten years, then fifteen years. By making excuses, I justified the feelings of failure. Eventually I had to let all excuses go and place the responsibility back on my shoulders.

I had to use this thing called faith in the Bible.

A THING CALLED FAITH

There's really no other way to live except by faith. All other ways fail to produce a complete life. Everything made by humans

> There's really no other way to live except by faith. All other ways fail to produce a complete life.

fails to produce fulfillment. Only a life of faith, living by faith and believing by faith, produces a fulfilled life.

> *For in it the righteousness of God is revealed from faith to faith; as it is written, "The just shall live by faith."* (Romans 1:17)

Faith is a strong belief in the spiritual or supernatural. It is a God-given trait and deep-seated need within every one of us, and we need it in order to blossom, to fulfill and expand our lives to the fullest.

> *The fundamental fact of existence is that this trust in God, this faith, is the firm foundation under everything that makes life worth living. It's our handle on what we can't see.* (Hebrews 11:1, MSG)

Everything in the Bible, from the life stories to the instructional teachings, points towards our need of faith to flourish. Everyone has something inside them they would like to see come to pass, things they believe will make them complete. We are created that way and encouraged to improve, expand, and produce.

Different theologians have taken different views on faith, but everyone can agree that faith is required to be successful.

The writer of the book of Hebrews explains that our hope in God and His Word can produce faith that creates a desired result. The most important thing to understand here is that we have a God who wants to partner and work with us to see our potential become reality, because only God has the power to accomplish the supernatural.

That's why I urge you to pray for absolutely everything, ranging from small to large. Include everything as you embrace this God-life, and you'll get God's everything. (Mark 11:24, MSG)

The desires we have inside us come from the Lord, and they may require change in us to see them fulfilled.

MAKE AN UNCOMPROMISING DECISION

Chi-Chi Rodríguez is a professional golfer who has won eight PGA titles. He once said, "Don't look for excuses to lose. Look for excuses to win."[10] Sometimes it means we have to make an uncompromising decision. When someone decides to be answerable for their choices, good or bad, they begin the progress towards change.

Responsibility is the quality of being responsible, answerable, and accountable. A responsible person is able to say, "I forgot," "I made a mistake," or "I shouldn't have done it that way." When we don't defend ourselves, we become people without excuse.

Change always requires work, but the result is the answer to an unfulfilled and unproductive life. Jesus explained how God's system works:

---

[10] *Inspiring Quotes*, "Chi Chi Rodriguez Quotes and Sayings." Date of access: September 25, 2017 (https://www.inspiringquotes.us/author/9784-chi-chi-rodriguez/page:3).

The Kingdom of God is like a farmer who scatters seed on the ground. Night and day, while he's asleep or awake, the seed sprouts and grows, but he does not understand how it happens. The earth produces the crops on its own. First a leaf blade pushes through, then the heads of wheat are formed, and finally the grain ripens. (Mark 4:26–28, NLT)

When someone begins the process of taking responsibility and not making excuses, it seems difficult or burdensome. At first sight, it might not even seem like the person is trying to change, but eventually, just like the seed, taking responsibility will become second mature. Others will take notice and see the competence, seeing a no-nonsense person.

Not making excuses will open doors that an excuse-filled life never could. It builds our confidence that with God's help we can accomplish anything. We can become highly productive people.

When we don't make excuses but take responsibility for our lives, does it mean we will never fail? Of course not, but we must know that failure is not defeat. Acknowledging failure is growth.

THE TIMES WE FAIL

Everyone needs to see that when they fail, they are not a failure in life. Anyone who has ever done anything of value has failed at one time or another. The only difference is that they never gave up and accepted failure. The failures only strengthened them and encouraged them to become successful. Some dictionaries define failure as an unsuccessful person. However, this definition is wrong; failure cannot be a way to identify ourselves.

Failing at something doesn't mean that the person is a failure. "Failure" cannot be a name we put on a person who has failed at something. They may have stumbled, but that does not make them a failure. When someone labels someone a failure, it implies that it's their character, who they are, yet when that person overcomes a defeat or disappointment they are not titled failures anymore.

It is not possible to ever define someone as a failure. A failure is simply a setback. When someone refuses to accept a failed attempt, they will begin to see results. It's important to know within yourself that you have not accepted failure. Only you can know if you have accepted failure, and many times this will reveal itself through excuses.

It doesn't matter if you desire to buy a house, be a stay at home mom, or become an executive in a corporation. These are all great accomplishments and everyone needs to decide for themselves whether they are wholeheartedly trying or making excuses. Again, excuses can be anything that stops you from trying to accomplish something, whether it's the first time or the third or fourth time.

NEVER TOO LATE

People have accomplished great things very late in life, even after a life of problems and failures. Harland David Sanders started the Kentucky Fried Chicken business at age sixty-five. Today the franchise exists in more than a hundred countries. Nelson Mandela was elected President of South Africa at the age of seventy-five.

The Bible includes numerous people who only began accomplishing great things very late in life. Moses and Aaron are examples. Moses had failed forty years earlier, yet he stood in front of the king of Egypt, attempting his most important assignment.

> *At the time when they spoke to the king, Moses was eighty years old, and Aaron was eighty-three.* (Exodus 7:7)

Abraham was a hundred years old when he began raising Isaac, who was in the bloodline of Jesus. Caleb and Joshua were between eighty and eighty-five years old when they finally began to make an impact. Joshua wrote that Caleb said, *"I was forty years old when the Lord's servant Moses sent me from Kadesh Barnea to spy out this land. I brought an honest report back to him"* (Joshua 14:7, GNT). Yet it was forty-five years later that he actually lived his dream of entering the Promised Land.

> **Failure is part of life and everyone needs to see it as taking a step forward, not backward.**

Failure is part of life and everyone needs to see it as taking a step forward, not backward. Failure shouldn't cause rejection. It's a process everyone goes through, yet somehow we forget our failures once we have success. All things considered, many successful people have had more failure than you and I have experienced, or will ever experience.

There is a psalm I like to recall every time I hit a wall or seem to fail at something:

The Lord guides us in the way we should go and protects those who please him. If they fall, they will not stay down, because the Lord will help them up. (Psalms 37:23–24, GNT)

God doesn't have a problem with failure. He loves to take failure and turn it into victory. God takes hurt and replaces it with healing. God takes sorrow and replaces it with joy. We may get knocked down, but we are never out unless we don't get up again. If you're looking for a good motto to replace an excuse, try this one: "I may have gotten knocked down but I am not out."

FUTURE TRUMPS PAST

Realizing that your past failures don't determine your future outcome is key. Everyone can recall times in life when they allowed failure to define them, only to come out the other side victorious. We can all think of times when we knew God stepped in and helped us. I like to remind myself about these past times. It helps when I'm in the middle of a failure.

You may be in the middle of a failure right now. Remember that it won't determine your end result. There is always time to recover. Failure disappoints me just as failure disappoints everyone, but everyone needs to see that God is on their side. He's not just sitting back watching, He's always working to get us to see where we could improve.

I can look back and remember times when I allowed myself to feel like a failure, times when I felt discouraged or thought life was disappointing. The thing that stopped me from giving up and accepting defeat was knowing that God cared about me. Then I would read something in the Bible that caused me to go on or I heard someone teach or preach an encouraging truth.

Sometimes when we're in a perceived failure, those thoughts trump the really valuable things of life. The things that should have priority can take a back seat as we struggle with our feelings. We begin to make excuses or worry about possible failures.

An important strategy is to always prioritize life.

PRIORITIES

Priorities have to do with how we think of things in their order of importance. Some things in life should be a higher priority than others. So many people have a constant struggle with priority issues. Money over family, position over honesty, sports before church. Everyone has a reason to justify their action, but mostly they are excuses. The real reason is not usually the one given.

Priorities begin to slip once someone fails to understand their role and importance. In overcoming an excuse-filled life, everyone must prioritize their lives according to the Bible. God doesn't demand priority in our lives, but He does ask us to see the importance of priority.

Priority is directly linked to an enjoyable life. When kept in proper order, everything else in life falls into place. Our main priorities are God, God's Word, family, vocation, and lastly our social lives. Everyone sets these main priorities differently. They may even sound out of order to you, but they are all directly linked to God's plan for our success.

GOD

Some people think God just wants control over us, because He's God. We are mere created beings who needs to know that we're nothing compared to Him. People think that's why He gave us a Bible with His do's and don'ts, to control us and put us in our place.

That logic fails to take into account the actual biblical explanation for life. The Bible should be used with the understanding that God had a purpose for creation. When the Bible is read in context, we see that God is not about rules and regulations; He is about family and the love of family. He is about helping us get to a place of peace and contentment, just as a father or mother wants their children to get to a place of peace and contentment.

We are created for a relationship with God that mainly benefits us. The writers of the Bible explain that God needs to be first place in our lives because of all the benefits this relationship produces. Without God, we try to manufacture our own benefits. The Old Testament shows mankind trying to manufacture its own benefits. The troubles and problems this produced caused God to step in before mankind destroyed itself. The New Testament is about the other side of this coin. With God in our lives, everything we need in life becomes accessible.

Seek the Kingdom of God above all else, and live righteously, and he will give you everything you need. (Matthew 6:33, NLT)

When the Bible tells us to live right and He will bless us, it sounds like a conditional offer. If you live for God, you get good things; if not, you get bad things. That's another misunderstanding of scripture. God knows that when we experience the goodness of a life with Him, veneration comes automatically. He doesn't need to demand it from us. God wants nothing to do with control and manipulation. When we allow God to take a key place in our lives, the other things we desire begin to fill in and we become whole.

This is exposed very clearly in the New Living Translation, which describes love like this:

Love is patient and kind. Love is not jealous or boastful or proud or rude. It does not demand its own way. It is not irritable, and it keeps no record of being wronged. It does not rejoice about injustice but rejoices whenever the truth wins out. Love never gives up, never loses faith, is always hopeful, and endures through every circumstance. (1 Corinthians 13:4–7, NLT)

True unconditional love would rather have a person make their own decision than force them to comply. This is the rationale of God and His desire for you, a true son or daughter. He offers us a free choice to belong to the best family ever to exist. It's your choice.

WORDS OF GOD

When we determine to live for God, we should automatically get to know what He has to say about things. When setting priorities, it's very important to allow for time in the Bible. Most people don't even realize that the scriptures are alive. By alive, I mean that they can speak to each of us, whenever we need guidance.

Instead of making excuses, we can know what the Bible says about a certain situation. We know that the Bible says we can be forgiven of any sin or failure. We know that God is always, always for us and never against us. Even if we mess up, He tells us in His Word that He is pulling for us to get back up and go forward.

What then shall we say to these things? If God is for us, who can be against us? (Romans 8:31)

The Bible also speaks to each of us about areas in our lives we might not easily see. Hebrews explains the Bible this way:

The word of God is alive and active, sharper than any double-edged sword. It cuts all the way through, to where soul and spirit meet, to where joints and marrow come together. It judges the desires and thoughts of the heart. (Hebrews 4:12, GNT)

This scripture speaks to the whole person being made well, spirit, soul and body. When dealing with priorities, the Bible should also have a significant place in our lives.

FAMILY

I like to go back to the record of creation, because at the beginning we can see God's heart. The way things were in the beginning is the way God always intended for things to be.

We can see that God is about family, so it stands to reason that family is a priority. Whether you have a large family or a small one, families need to stay together as best they can. Of course, we know that God gave mankind the power of choice, and the choices they made over time disrupted the original plan. However, even though the original intent for family is confused today, with so many blended and scattered families, God has never changed His mind. Families were His intention from the very beginning.

So God created human beings, making them to be like himself. He created them male and female, blessed them, and said, "Have many children, so that your descendants will live all over the earth and bring it under their control. I am putting you in charge of the fish, the birds, and all the wild animals." (Genesis 1:27–28, GNT)

The Lord God said, "It isn't good for the man to live alone. I need to make a suitable partner for him." (Genesis 2:18, CEV)

We can also see numerous instructions where God asks the whole family to look out for each other. Here is one such example:

Wives, understand and support your husbands by submitting to them in ways that honor the Master. Husbands, go all out in love for your wives. Don't take advantage of them. Children, do what your parents tell you. This delights the Master no end. Parents, don't come down too hard on your children or you'll crush their spirits. (Colossians 3:18–21, MSG)

No family is perfect, and each family has unique circumstances, but making family a priority begins to narrow down our responsibilities. Instead of making excuses about why we cannot make something work in our families, we need to be able to see the goodness each part of the family brings.

VOCATION

This priority often takes first place, and it's usually an area of contention, requiring a great balancing act. God wants His kids to be successful, and some vocations require more time than others. God wants people to be good at what they do and they should be profitable. These are all biblical principles.

However, when a person's vocation ends up being about financial security, status, and satisfaction, then excuses emerge. These things become of such importance in someone's thinking that they're willing to sacrifice time with God and their families to succeed at their job. Eventually, this practice can produce a workaholic.

Workaholics are in bondage and value any kind of work over other priorities. When a person's vocation takes first place, their relationships with God, His Word, and the family all take a back seat. They use their occupation to gain acceptance, recognition, and support. They have lost trust in God, and the encouragement of family, in an attempt to do things on their own. This is where having a complete balance of God, family, and work becomes the catalyst to destroying excuses.

SOCIAL

A person's social life is mentioned last in the list of priorities because it can drive us to making the most impractical excuses. In our world today, filled with technology, social media, and reality shows, we tend to make enjoyment and entertainment the focus of our lives. Entertainment can become a time thief, stealing our time from other priorities. Someone once said, "Save the excuses. It's not about having time, it's about making time. If something matters, you will make time."

God advises us to use time properly. Only when people have grown old and looked back over their lives will they fully understand the gravity of wasted time. Now, I'm not saying that entertainment is all wasted time—everyone must rejuvenate and have some periods of rest—but once we begin to shortchange the higher prioritizes of life in favor of our social lives, we undermine our own joy.

Psalm 90 was written by Moses, who lived to be one hundred and twenty years. He wrote,

Teach us to use wisely all the time we have.
(Psalms 90:12, CEV)

CONCLUSION

WHEN I FIRST RECEIVED THE INTERPRETATION OF THE WORD "fragile" from the Lord, I knew this was real. These frailties are actually weaknesses. They are extreme feelings that have manipulated me. Fear, rejection, anxiety, guilt, intimidation, lies, and excuses have all played a role in forming my character—and it's out of character with the person I could be. These things influenced the real me, keeping me bound up.

As Paul reminded us, *"For we are His workmanship, created in Christ Jesus for good works, which God prepared beforehand that we should walk in them"* (Ephesians 2:10). When I began to see this, my first reaction was that I needed healing from the frailties that held me back. If I could get healed of these things, I could begin to change.

This, again, was wrong thinking.

If there is one thing I really wanted to say as I wrote this book, it's that overcoming unhealthy thoughts is not a matter of just getting healed of them. We don't find any evidence in the Bible that God will overrule our emotions and feelings. God does not exert any of His power over us other than through His Word, which is the Bible or the Holy Spirit speaking within us.

> If there is one thing I really wanted to say as I wrote this book, it's that overcoming unhealthy thoughts is not a matter of just getting healed of them.

There are some things God cannot do for us, because He gave us a free will to believe whatever we want to believe. God will protect us, prosper us, and guide our lives. He will help us to change spiritually, mentally, and physically. However, the power to choose what we believe is ours. The power to decide and act or react is ours.

This all stems from our thinking, and our thinking affects our beliefs. God gave us the responsibility, or the free will, to believe or disbelieve. Even as you read this book, you have a right to believe or disbelieve the contents. It's up to you.

Overthrowing these influences in our lives is first a matter of seeing them and second a matter of taking responsibility for them. God didn't give them to us, nor did anyone force them on us; we accepted them over time and now we need to start changing them. It is our responsibility, of course, with God's help and the guidance of the Holy Spirit. This is going to require us to make regular observations of what and how we feel.

Until we reach eternity, there will never be an end to the opportunities for fear and worry. There will always be occasions to be intimidated and rejected. There will be ample reasons to make excuses or believe a lie. That's just life. However, once we have a grip on these feelings, we will begin to see the advantage of taking authority over them.

TAKE AUTHORITY

Let me remind you that these patterns, attitudes, and beliefs are more than just mistakes. They might have begun as mistakes on our part, because we accepted them without resistance—and other people may have played a part in trying to make us believe them—but they have gained influence in us because we have misunderstood their power over us.

How these beliefs came to be is a footnote. Knowing that they have grown into an unnatural power is of crucial importance. When I say unnatural power, I mean that they are not natural to people. God never created them to overwhelm our lives.

What has transpired is that people have allowed themselves to accept artificial truth. Artificial truth is false truth that doesn't come from inside, where a person's spirit lives; it comes from the mental realm. The ruler of the kingdom of darkness, satan, had a part to play in causing us to embrace wrong beliefs.

These artificial thoughts do not come from God. Refuse to agree with the notion that you have to accept what your wrong feelings tell you. Feelings can be arrested, held back, taken into custody. The effects of fear, rejection, anxiety, guilt, intimidation, lies, and excuses can be captured so that you can reach the goals you desire. If you don't make the connection that they have a role to play in shaping your feelings, then overcoming them will be impossible.

LET THE WEAK SAY I AM STRONG

A powerful tool in fighting wrong thoughts is speaking words to oneself. The Bible says that David encouraged himself. When he was afraid, He spoke, *"I trust in God and am not afraid; I praise him for what he has promised. What can a mere human being do to me?"* (Psalms 56:4, GNT)

When we are being overcome by wrong thoughts, use scripture. That's why God has spoken to us through the Bible. Use scriptures to speak to yourself:

...He who is in you is greater than he who is in the world. (1 John 4:4, MKJV)

But in all these things we more than conquer through Him who loved us. (Romans 8:37, MKJV)

I can do all things through Christ who strengthens me. (Philippians 4:13, MKJV)

Sometimes no one is around to encourage us. At times people can't or won't take the time to see what's happening in our lives. Every so often people don't catch on to what we're feeling. On occasion, no one cares.

Be like David and say to yourself, "I am God's child. I have been redeemed. I am forever forgiven. I am born of God."

PARTNERSHIP

Partnership is relationship. Relationship is trust. Learning to trust in God is a trait we need to developed. When we step out to conquer a wrong thought, it will never be easy. Each time wrong thoughts try to attach themselves to us, it will be a battle—and it will take time. Each opportunity is a battle and each victory builds confidence.

We must trust God for everything in our lives. When we see effective results, we need to recognize that it was God's hand in our lives helping to give us the victory. We must go through a phase of trusting God, which is always easier said than done, but nevertheless it is required. Even today, trust God to be part of what you're doing. Believe in Psalms 25:2:

O my God, I trust in You; do not let me be ashamed, let not my enemies triumph over me. (MKJV)

Trust God for the outcome of any situation.

SALVATION

Having read this whole book will help, to a degree, but more is needed. You need a relationship with Jesus Christ. You will not have lasting power over these fragilities without truly knowing Jesus as Savior. Arriving at this higher place will require a relationship that is called "regeneration"—or, as others have put it, being born again. Jesus confirmed this in John 3, saying, *"Humans give life to their children. Yet only God's Spirit can change you into a child of God"* (John 3:6, CEV).

God sent someone to rescue us, but again, it's a choice. It requires not only a belief that Jesus existed, but you have to put your trust and life in His hands. If you have recognized and are regretful that you have sinned and want to change, you need help.

It is possible to live guilt-free from sin. However, many people have tried to change on their own. The truth still stands.

Salvation is to be found through him alone; in all the world there is no one else whom God has given who can save us. (Acts 4:12, GNT)

Of course, we know this to be Jesus. You must be willing to trust in Jesus, who promises to forgive you. You must trust in Him who promises to never leave or abandon you. He wants to be on your side no matter what happens. He is willing to work with you to make you a conquering success.

Do you want to live through eternity with God? Then you need to make a commitment, from the heart, and use words:

God, I need help. I cannot be the person I should be. I sin and make mistakes. I want to change. I ask You, Jesus, to forgive and redeem me. Jesus, You are my only hope. Please come into my life and set me free. Thank You. I will live for You to the best of my ability. I will learn of You and give You first place in my life. Thank You that I am Your child. Amen.

www.myking.ca

IS HERE FOR ONE REASON AND ONE REASON ONLY. TO HELP people connect with God and reach their full potential. We get excited when we hear someone truly say 'I know Him'. A lot of Christians only know about salvation into heaven, but Jesus has provided so much more. More for everyday life, everyday challenges and everyday happiness. It is our desire at 'My King Ministries' to see that every Christian walks in the fullness and supernatural benefits available through Jesus Christ. We teach the Word of God in a relevant and inspiring way. Bringing biblical insights into becoming healthy, vibrant and strong. We would love for you to be part of this growing ministry.

To contact B. T. Semeschuk through 'My King Ministries'

Visit: www.myking.ca
Write: Box 233, Red Deer, Alberta, Canada, T4N 5E8
Email: info@myking.ca
Text or call: 403-885-5797